The Country Garden

The Country Garden

TRISHA DIXON

Angus&Robertson
An imprint of HarperCollins*Publishers*

AN ANGUS & ROBERTSON BOOK
An imprint of HarperCollinsPublishers

First published in Australia in 1992 by
CollinsAngus&Robertson Publishers Pty Limited (ACN 009 913 517)
A division of HarperCollinsPublishers (Australia) Pty Limited
25-31 Ryde Road, Pymble NSW 2073, Australia

HarperCollinsPublishers (New Zealand) Limited
31 View Road, Glenfield, Auckland 10, New Zealand

HarperCollinsPublishers Limited
77-85 Fulham Palace Road, London W6 8JB, United Kingdom

Distributed in the United States of America by
HarperCollinsPublishers
10 East 53rd Street, New York NY 10022, USA

National Library of Australia
Cataloguing-in-Publication data:

Dixon, Trisha, 1953-

   The country garden.

   ISBN 0 207 17481 4.

   1. Gardens - Design. 2. Gardening 3. Vegetable gardening.
   4. Landscape gardening. I. Title.

712.6

Typeset by Midland Typesetters, Maryborough
Printed in Hong Kong

  1 2 3 4 5
96 95 94 93 92

CONTENTS: *The art of growing flowering plants at the water's edge makes them seem at home in their setting, as do these flowering Hostas.*

To my parents, whose joyful exuberance of life is my inspiration.

CONTENTS

CONTENTS

INTRODUCTION

The image of the country garden is so evocative, with its abundance of flowers, sense of mystery, and incomparable vistas, that it is little wonder that urban dwellers are now emulating this country look in gardens throughout the towns and cities of the world. Most gardeners have their own unique image of the 'ideal' country garden. Images recalled from holidays in the country, childhood recollections, nostalgic reminiscences and pastoral impressions become indelibly stamped on our memory. Perhaps it is an inherent love of all things country — the yearning for a simpler life.

A feeling of relaxed informality is the essence of the country garden. This is not the type of garden where particular styles or modes are slavishly imitated. It is the guiding hand that nurtures and tends the garden that creates the intended nirvana. There are many styles *within* the country garden and many styles *of* country garden. There are no limits — no rigid guidelines.

Creating a garden style draws heavily on intuitive images. You may study Botany, memorise Latin names and delve into plant knowledge, but it is the *placing* of these plants that will create the garden's style. The shelves of libraries and bookshelves throughout the world embody reams of advice to assist the gardener, yet in our knowledge we may know too much. It is our own intuitive, artistic nature that must shine through the science. We must use our surroundings as an artist uses a canvas. Nothing too technical, or too clever, to appear contrived, but that subtle blend of knowledge and aesthetics, practicalities with mystique, and capabilities with philosophy. As an art form, creating a garden is perhaps the most complex of all. It is not a static art, and so needs foresight, faith, fair weather and firm resolve!

This book is for the many gardeners who have all of the above qualities in abundance, but are still seeking visual images to fashion corners of their own country garden; or for those ensconced in suburbia who dream of life on the farm.

TRISHA DIXON
'BOBUNDARA'

LEFT: Early spring in the wild garden at Bobundara, with the first sign of green on the elms after a long, cold winter.

PLANNING THE GARDEN

Design on paper is one thing—it is another to transform ideas and plans into reality. Being disciplined enough to create a unified look requires firm resolve.

DESIGN

ABOVE: Scale is a vital consideration in the country garden. The size of the house needs to be in proportion to the type of garden. Large houses need trees that will grow to great heights and larger expanses of lawn than smaller cottages.

OPPOSITE: An important aspect in design is taking into consideration plants for particular effects. The brilliant tones of the ornamental grape are a highlight of autumn in cool climate gardens.

PREVIOUS PAGES: This subtle planting association of blues and creams creates a tranquil corner in which to rest and survey the garden.

In the changing canvas of the countryside, the garden is only part of the whole vista. The rural backdrop sets the scene and may be incorporated in the garden design. Distant vistas may be 'borrowed', adding depth and interest to the smallest of gardens. Natural features may be incorporated, such as streams or ponds, and natural materials may be utilised in the architecture of the garden. Local stone may be used for walls or paving and existing vegetation may form a starting point for the planting.

Design is paramount to the success of any garden. It is the art of beautifying our surroundings to our own style. A garden without any semblance of design need not, however, be a catastrophe. One only has to walk in the bush where the intrinsic beauty of natural planting is unparalleled. Trying to emulate this natural look is, however, far harder than it would seem. Once the ground has been disturbed to build a house, garage and outbuildings, there is an imbalance between the natural

ABOVE: Part of the art of design is keeping planting complementary to the style of building. Old buildings may be wonderfully complemented by the simplest plants, such as this red japonica which provides a splash of colour late in winter.

OPPOSITE: Using space well is just as important to a garden as selecting the right plants. The open lawn in front of this house is restful in its simplicity.

and artificial—weeds flourish and added foliage is often needed to camouflage the man-made structures.

This is where design plays an important role. A creative design may either unify the surroundings or provide an architectural framework distinct from the backdrop. Design need not necessarily be structured, but it takes out the disparity and inconsistency that may come from thinking only of plants. A strong design gives that vital structure that will help carry a

garden through the vagaries of a country existence—dry summers, frosty winters, winds, droughts and snow.

Design on paper is one thing—it is another to transform ideas and plans into reality. Being disciplined enough to create a unified look, rather than dotting trees and shrubs bought on impulse in any available space, requires firm resolve. In design, the spaces are just as important as the plants. I feel this is the most commonly made mistake when planning gardens—not

ABOVE: Nature provides a wonderful helping hand to the art of creating a garden.
The beauty of the moss on this path blends in subtly with the surrounding foliage.
ABOVE RIGHT: Rustic gates, mossy stones and antiquated furniture add to the
ambience of the country garden.
OPPOSITE: The beauty of architecture in the garden. These stately columns look
wonderful swathed in the abundant greenery of the ornamental grape.

taking into consideration that wonderful feeling of space. Too often trees and shrubs are dotted haphazardly with little thought to their arrangement and eventual height. Even in the smallest of gardens, garden rooms may be created by thoughtful design and planting.

Design principles may be applied to established gardens just as they are for beginning a garden from scratch. Eliminating or opening up areas or vistas may often be the making of established gardens, not forgetting that there must be an ongoing tree planting scheme for future generations. A disparate garden may be unified by broad brushstrokes of one plant or colour, adding a path or wall, or creating an accent or focal point. Hedges lend a unifying appearance to a garden, while pergolas or avenues lead the eye onwards and may link different parts of the garden. Symmetry may be emphasised by neat clipped edges or hedging; or softened by rampant planting.

Scale is a significant detail, particularly when considering the home and outbuildings so associated with the country garden. Imposing buildings need to be balanced by sizable trees. The width of paths, height of walls and expanse of lawns need to be in proportion to the house, creating a feeling of unity. Hugh

Johnson writes that unity is the ideal that is very rarely reached—at least by amateur gardeners. 'There are too many temptations to wander into irrelevant and distracting by-ways. Every magazine article that makes you form a mental picture of another "feature" in your garden is the voice of the devil. Unfortunately it is new features that give most gardeners most fun.'

Set your own style and try not to be distracted by passing fads and too many ideas from magazines and garden visits! Most importantly, make this style achievable. Set yourself sensible

BELOW: Restrained use of plant material imparts an elegance in keeping with the architecture of the house and expansive garden.

OPPOSITE: The very simplicity of the Erigeron planted at the foot of this sculpture, and the vast background of lawn bounded by a low stone wall, adds to the air of restfulness in this country garden.

FOLLOWING PAGES: It is really only in the larger expanses of the country garden that such wonderful effects may be achieved with daffodils, here naturalised on the bank of a river.

limits. I am one of the greatest offenders for extending the garden fence—however not for more garden beds, only to open views. If the garden is too large, create your own manageable boundary with a low stone wall, hedge or shrubbery and let the rest go *au naturel*. If you feel your garden to be too diminutive, open up views and let the surrounding countryside be your own 'no-care' garden.

It was John Brookes who said that 'gardens should be very small or you will have no fun at all!' However there are small gardens and there are small gardens. This is where design plays an all important role. A cleverly designed small garden which incorporates the greater visage of the landscape beyond may be immeasurably enhanced. An effective means of having a seemingly large expanse of garden with relatively little upkeep is to confine the garden beds to the perimeters of the house and use a low wall or hedge to delineate a boundary. Weeding, watering and mowing need only be carried out in this 'cultivated' area within the boundary. A large area may then extend beyond this boundary, planted with shade trees and any surplus bulbs from the garden. This area need not be sown with lawn, but

may be mown occasionally to keep from becoming too unkempt. Not only will this give the effect of expanding the garden's borders but may serve as a shady parking area.

Two country gardens I greatly admire are both relatively small, but their strong design characteristics and uninterrupted views to the countryside beyond, leave an indelible impression. One is totally enclosed by a stone wall, high at the sides and back to provide much needed protection from strong winds and frosts, and low at the front to enable an uninterrupted view of the pastoral scene of grazing sheep and cattle and distant hills beyond. Focus in this garden lies with the wonderful vista and pleasing sense of design. The other garden has a sloping lawn running down to a semi-circular ha-ha wall, giving unimpeded views of the surrounding countryside. In both these gardens, plants play second fiddle to the overall visage.

Plants play an important role in personalising the garden; their selection and maintenance will give the garden its own identity. Old fashioned roses, hollyhocks and foxgloves will lend an old-world atmosphere that may tone down a modern home or informalise an imposing domicile. Native flora will blend the garden into the surroundings, while a garden emphasising productive trees and plants imparts an air of practicality suited to the country environment. A garden of trees and lawns is restful and significantly more manageable than an area devoted wholly to flowers and shrubs.

Time is the essence. Be realistic: maintain your priorities and objectives. If it is imperative to have fresh fruit and vegetables, don't let the kitchen garden take second place to the flower beds. If cooking is your great passion, perhaps the herb garden may be the focal point of the garden. If time is limited, either reduce your expectations or come to terms with a wilder, more informal style of gardening. Gardens are to be enjoyed, and as Shelley said, 'to give happiness and repose of mind'.

LEFT: Foxgloves, buttercups and the red flowering Salvia grahamii *are all prolific in their flowering and growth habits and create an enchanting picture together.*
OPPOSITE: Coming to terms with the surroundings is much of the secret to country gardening. Rather than obliterating pastoral scenes such as this one of sheep grazing, vistas may be incorporated into the garden's boundaries as 'borrowed landscapes'.

UNDERSTANDING THE SITE

ABOVE: The inimitable beauty of water in the garden. The attraction here lies in the natural setting, with the stream meandering through an uncontrived planting of elms.

Local knowledge is critical in understanding and managing the country garden. Without it, years may be wasted in trial and error. Coming to terms with a particular climate and soil type is often not something that may be read from a book but is gleaned by talking to neighbours, visiting other gardens in the area and by being receptive to local lore.

This does not necessarily mean one is tied to a particular set of rules. Whatever the soil type, it may be greatly enhanced and restructured with the addition of compost, fertiliser and additives. Acid soil may be normalised by liberal applications of lime, while heavy clay soil may be made more manageable with gypsum, peat moss or well rotted sawdust. Having tested the pH of the soil in your garden and found that it is distinctly alkaline, take advantage of the lavenders, carnations, sweet peas and tulips that will flourish, but don't despair of growing acid-loving azaleas which will flourish at the base of pine trees.

Similarly, if frosts are too severe to grow that special plant that you covet, try growing it against a wall in a sheltered position, under the canopy of an established tree in a protected corner, or in a tub in a courtyard or verandah. There is great flexibility in gardening and throughout the centuries, gardeners have challenged the elements by finding the means to grow plants whatever the climate or soil conditions.

Climatic conditions, more than soil type, limits a gardener's choice in plants. Cool climate gardeners should revel in the autumn colours, bulbs, berries, apples and stone fruit that flourish in the cooler temperatures rather than pine for the lusher, more tropical plants. How I have always longed to grow french lavender (*Lavandula dentata*) with its plump soft heads when I should be content with the green, white, pink and mauve english lavender that thrives in our cold climate.

Many plant lovers will have been lured by evocative plant catalogues or tempting nurseries while holidaying in far flung locations, only to find most of these impulse buys turn up their heels after only one season. This is not to put away thoughts of experimentation. It is a gardener's prerogative to want to try growing something novel. The joy of discovery and pleasure in the unknown is much of the delight in gardening; waiting for an unknown bloom to burst open or for cuttings to bud. Avid readers are always writing lists of plants to look out for and garden visitors need a notebook at hand to jot down names. Visiting gardens with a similar climate is a great learning experience and much may be gained by talking to the owners of gardens you admire or to local nursery owners.

Temperature fluctuations limit a garden's range of plants to a far greater extent than water, soil types or wind. Coming to terms with a garden's limitations in terms of the elements that *can't* be controlled is not an overnight phenomenon. There is always the challenge to try something that will defy the elements. The controlling factor is ultimately the frequency, severity and duration of frost. Most gardens can withstand an occasional frost, but where frosts are a common occurrence for most of the year, plants need to be carefully selected and cultivated to maximise frost resistance.

Learning to accept and delight in the range of plants suited to your own climatic conditions leads on to designing the garden to greatest advantage. Shade trees are paramount in a hot climate, while deciduous trees allow the penetration of winter sun in cool climates. Planting trees with an eye for the future is not easy. It is hard for most gardeners to assess the size of a tree's canopy ten to thirty years later.

Strong winds can distress many country gardeners, necessitating windbreaks, fences, walls and hedges. Winds not only dry out the garden considerably, they reduce temperatures, defoliate trees and exasperate all within! For immediate relief, fast-growing wind tolerant trees can be grown in strategic places throughout the garden. Evergreen wind-resistant plants include *Viburnum tinus, Eucalyptus, Melia azederach, Casuarina* spp, *Abelia grandiflora, Feijoa sellowiana,* olive, chinese elm, and the brush box.

Rainfall is not the limitation it once was before watering systems, pumps and bores. However, in the large expanse of the country garden, it is hard to sustain large areas of water-loving plants in arid areas. Far better to choose plants that thrive in the hot dry conditions, mulching well to conserve moisture. Most Australian native plants are suited to dry conditions, as

ABOVE: What better 'borrowed landscape' than a field of buttercups—often too rampant for the garden beds, but quite a picture en masse. *Rustic wooden gates lend much to the atmosphere of the perimeter of the country garden.*

are the lavenders, herbs, salvias, strelitzias, statice, marigolds, daylilies, pelargonium, Jerusalem sage, nasturtiums, cosmos, daisies, yarrow and achillea.

Living in a dry climate, it is hard to imagine needing to choose plants specifically for damp areas, but many gardeners have a constant battle with an excess of moisture. Poor drainage areas may also be enhanced by moisture-loving plants such as ferns, mosses and rainforest type plants. Some trees are not only adapted to wet areas but also absorb excess water. These

LEFT: A natural feature such as a river or stream provides a focal point that requires little gilding. Understanding the site may mean working out the flood level of nearby creeks or rivers and keeping the garden border above this level.

ABOVE: Frequent mists and fogs provide added moisture for the garden and cast an ethereal aura over the garden.

FOLLOWING PAGES: The simplicity of the country garden: an old stone wall, drifts of daffodils and a cottage.

include the silver birch, willow bottlebrush, swamp banksia, black wattle, swamp cypress, river red gum, Nyssa tupelo, Pin oak, tortured willow, swamp mahogany and golden elm.

Perhaps one of the gardener's most useful tools is a notebook where plant names may be recorded—plants to look out for, names of plants or cuttings given by friends, plants purchased and gardening tips. Gardening lore passed on by friends and gardening acquaintances often has greater local relevance than general horticultural knowledge.

ABOVE: Merging the perimeter of the garden with the surrounding countryside has greater appeal than an abrupt end to the garden. Here, hardy iris look wonderful rising from a swathe of unmown grass.

OPPOSITE: Vistas of the countryside beyond add much to the garden's atmosphere, particularly in the country garden where distant hills add to the sense of scale and breadth of a garden.

BORROWED
LANDSCAPES

Images of the countryside beyond are the making of many a country garden. To visually extend the garden into the distance lends immense breadth and depth. A small garden is infinitely enlarged by incorporating the country beyond, particularly in the rural landscape where there is a fresh pastoral naturalness that has a beauty far surpassed by man-made horticultural plots.

Too often, country gardens are enclosed within their own boundaries, blocking off any glimpses of vistas beyond. This has not always been planned, but rather evolved over decades, as trees mature to gargantuan heights little expected by those

ABOVE: This peaceful expanse of water provides a subtle boundary between the garden and the countryside beyond.

OPPOSITE: Gardens that flow into the countryside beyond, with glimpses of grazing stock and farm sheds, have a wonderful simplicity. Excess bulbs from within the garden may be planted to great effect along the garden's perimeter.

who planted a diminutive seedling. One of the gardener's most soul-wrenching chores is removing established trees that have taken years of nurturing. However, the removal of just one tree may open up the garden to the beauty of the countryside beyond, enhancing the garden immeasurably. This effectively allows the ambience of the countryside to permeate the garden.

A glimpse may be just as pleasing as an entire panorama, depending on the site and scale of the garden. Framing a view may heighten one aspect of the rural backdrop and effectively screen blots in the landscape. Wind direction is an important

consideration when removing existing trees and large hedges. Letting in howling winds to a previously sheltered garden may take much from the peaceful atmosphere, however wonderful the view.

Integrating the landscape into the garden means camouflaging the boundaries so that one may flow into the other. The most effective way of doing this is with a ha-ha fence—a low retaining wall or sunken ditch not visible from the garden. Ha-ha fences have been used for centuries as a way of allowing the garden to flow into the countryside. In the country, more than anywhere,

RIGHT: *River Red Gums,*
Eucalyptus camaldulensis, *are*
among the most stately of the
Australian gums, making a
spectacular natural backdrop to
this country garden.

aesthetics must be outweighed by practicalities. It is all very well to have a stunning view with an impractical low wall or timber rail fence, but if it does not serve as a deterrent to grazing stock in the adjacent paddock, it is futile. The widespread use of electric fencing has great advantages on the outer perimeters of a garden if used judiciously. One electric wire running out from the structure is enough to thoroughly deter any capricious stock.

Low stone walls not only lend atmosphere to the garden but do not distract the eye when used as a barrier between garden and rural backdrop. There is something venerable and pastoral about a stone wall that is so in tune with the country garden atmosphere. Dry or mortared, they create a natural barrier in empathy with the surrounding countryside. Rustic wooden and brushwood woven fencing provides a low impact barrier and needs little maintenance. Practical wire fencing may be camouflaged with greenery so as not to draw attention to its presence. Traditionally, local materials are used to create such boundaries. This provides a link between garden and rural backdrop and echoes the feeling of the countryside.

OUTDOOR ROOMS

Interest in a garden is considerably heightened with subtle enclosures of greenery. To wander down leafy pathways to secluded areas of the garden is one of the joys of discovering or appreciating a garden. The garden becomes an extension of the house, providing intimate outdoor living areas.

To see the garden in one sweep takes away the delight of exploration. Much of the pleasure of visiting a garden is in the anticipation of what lies beyond. There is also a wonderful warm feeling of envelopment when entering a concealed enclosure of greenery. Anyone who has read that great classic *The Secret Garden* by Frances Hodgson Burnett will understand this wonderment of discovery.

Edna Walling wrote 'One always hopes to find a garden full of surprises', and there is no doubt that her design skills were utilised to the full in creating a series of outdoor rooms in the smallest of gardens. 'There is a mistaken idea that if the area is small it must on no account be broken up for fear it will appear even more limited. The smaller the area the more imperative it becomes to devise some means of making it appear larger. To do this, we must conceal the boundaries as much as possible, and break up the remainder with groups of trees and shrubs which form vistas, creating a sense of distance which does not really exist.'

While scale is an important aspect of the country garden, with distant vistas lending breadth and interest, enclosed areas create that enticing sense of mystery. A garden that lingers long in the memory is a garden with a soul. This need not necessarily be a garden of any great horticultural excellence or one with rare and exotic plants, rather a garden that is enveloped in a veil of enchantment. A garden where it is possible to walk along each path without ever having to retrace your steps; a garden of surprises and natural beauty. Gardens that are too contrived lose this romantic allure, despite their horticultural brilliance.

RIGHT: The profuse blooms of Fortuneana *provide a welcoming entrance.*

OPPOSITE: A feeling of intimacy exists in this beautifully tended garden room, with its welcoming seat setting, dry stone wall boundary and wonderfully bounteous plantings of old-fashioned perennials.

ABOVE: In the country garden, harmony is the key and garden seating needs to be carefully selected and positioned. Ideally any garden furniture should blend in rather than demand centre stage.

LEFT: A feeling of intimacy exists in this garden room, where pleached limes make a shady canopy with Lilium regale growing in the filtered shade.

OPPOSITE: No matter how small the area, gardens may be divided into 'rooms', creating greater visual effect and interest than a garden that can be surveyed in one glance. Here, slight changes in level and border planting create distinct garden rooms with great effect.

FOLLOWING PAGES: Geraniums in terracotta pots are a classic country favourite, brightening up a sunny window-sill.

One of the most charming gardens I have ever visited, and never fail to be captivated by, is the Micalago Station garden, seen by many in that Australian film classic, *My Brilliant Career*. One of Australia's oldest gardens, its charm lies in its collection of original buildings enclosing small areas of lawn and garden, forming a series of garden rooms. Simple plants have been used to great effect, adding to the feeling of nostalgia and history that pervades the garden; proving more successful than a collection of rare plants, that would be more inclined to distract the eye and draw attention to themselves.

There are no hard and fast rules for creating garden rooms, except that they should be attuned to the mood of the garden. An informal country garden is more suited to walls of greenery, with an eclectic mixture of trees, shrubs, bulbs and perennials forming boundaries, or walls draped in greenery; whereas more classical country gardens may utilise an architectural framework of formal stone or brick walls, tall hedges or avenues of trees.

A mixture of evergreen and deciduous trees and shrubs, with broad brushstrokes of foliage colour, create year-round interest. As in all plant selection, it is vital to look at plants with an eye to having something of interest throughout the year. This transition of focus throughout the seasons sets a note of change in the garden. It is then on closer inspection that the more subtle beauty of leaves, limbs and foliage are discovered.

The country garden is generally the focal point of the owners entertainment, with large stretches of lawn used for games of cricket or croquet, shady trees to eat under and paths for children to ride bicycles and play hide-and-seek along. Kitchens opening onto leafy terraces and into shady courtyards provide additional outdoor rooms throughout the warm summer months, while in the cooler months it is tempting to have a well-positioned seat in a sheltered area to enjoy the winter sun.

SETTING THE STYLE

Garden style is intensely personal. It is an expression of the gardener's own artistic inclinations and ambitions.

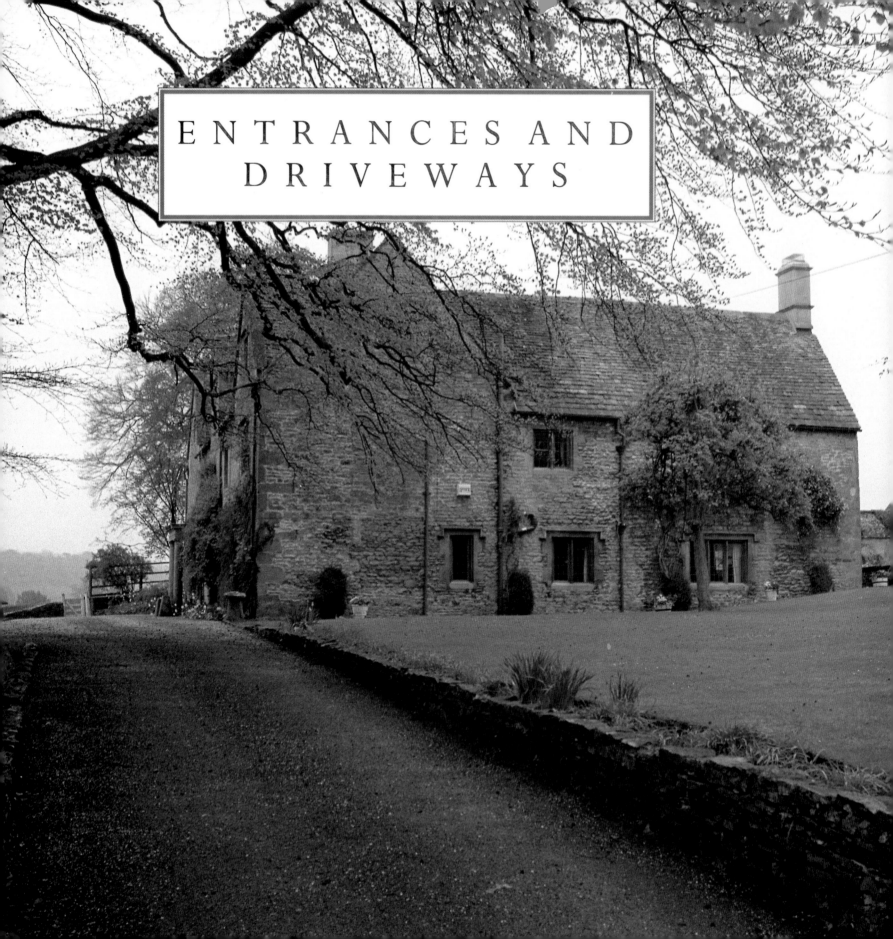

ENTRANCES AND DRIVEWAYS

ABOVE: Prunus serrulata 'Kanzan' brightens the entrance to this country garden.
OPPOSITE: There is much to be said in favour of the understated entrance, relying not so much on the grandeur of the entrance as the garden within—in this case, with its rustic building and towering trees providing atmosphere in abundance.

The entrance to a country property or garden gives the first impression of what lies beyond and so needs careful consideration. Too grand an entrance may lead to unreal expectations, whereas an unassuming approach lends a sense of anticipation. There is something alluring in a modest entrance as there are then no false expectations. Delight is heightened if the garden is beyond expectations. My general impression is that the plainer the

entrance, the more enticing the garden beyond—whereas grand entrances often lead to disappointments within!

The approach to a country garden is vastly different to a town garden entrance. Often situated kilometres away from the garden, perhaps the most unassuming way to announce an entrance is with trees. If there is an abundance of local stone, a dressed or dry stone low wall forms a solid entrance. Timber gates have a rural ambience which is soon lost when too much white paint is splashed around. Miles of white fencing tends to be overkill, but a more sympathetic colour or timber stain is in harmony with the surrounding countryside.

The further the house and garden is from the front entrance, the more understated the entrance needs to be. If the garden is out of sight from the road, a massive structure may be an overstatement, unless an avenue of trees leads from the entrance to the garden. However, if the garden extends to the front road entrance, a large entrance against a backdrop of greenery is not as conspicuous. Using trees that echo the natural vegetation is a way of playing down an entrance with great effect.

Landscape designers differ greatly in their views of front entrances, some opting for the simple approach while others prefer the grand statement. Edna Walling wrote on the charm of the simple entrance. 'A drive that runs over the landscape in easy sweeping curves, following as natural a track as possible and where the cattle and sheep may graze right up to the very edge of the roadway, generally fits into the landscape much more harmoniously than one that is laboriously planted and maintained.' Where there is little native growth or interest in contour, she believed an avenue of trees is a suitable alternative.

As in all gardening, the matter of driveway design is intensely personal and to a great extent reflects the taste of the person

LEFT: These large elms carpet the drive with golden leaves in autumn and provide an overture to the elms in the garden beyond.

OPPOSITE: A traditional wooden field gate provides an understated entrance to this magnificent garden.

within. In reality, most country garden entrances are inherited and it is only those starting afresh that have the opportunity to create anew.

Two of the most stunning driveways I have seen have a natural planting of Australian eucalypts to announce the approach. One of these is the much photographed entrance to Dame Elisabeth Murdoch's Cruden Farm garden in Victoria, where lemon-scented gums (*Eucalyptus citriodora*) are planted in an informal sweeping curve from the simple field gate to the home. The other is the approach to a garden known for its wonderful

daffodil collection. Overflows from the garden have been planted amongst the native eucalypts, completely in harmony with its rural setting and simply charming in its natural simplicity.

For those starting afresh, critically appraise all the entrances you pass on drives in the country and decide what it is that appeals most to your sensibility. Photograph, sketch or take notes of ones that appeal most and take it from there—not copying, but collating ideas for your own individual entrance. Relate the front entrance to an overture; setting the scene and providing a link between the entrance, countryside and garden beyond.

GARDEN BUILDINGS

ABOVE: The historic buildings which bound this gravel forecourt give an indication to the visitor of the age of the garden beyond.

OPPOSITE: Grape underplanted with pink valerian provides a welcome entrance to this farm building.

These may often be the making of a country garden—old brick stables, or an antiquated aviary; an old summer-house or stone barn. These instantly lend atmosphere and add that other dimension that even ingenious planting may not achieve. How often have you seen an old farm building totally neglected and unused in its present site that would look marvellous at the bottom of your garden!

An old thatched roof potting shed or wooden slab dairy would be a wonderful addition, but don't despair when the reality is an old garden shed badly in need of paint. Even a ghastly fibro shed can be given a facelift by covering it with weatherboards. A windvane may add a whimsical air and a window spilling over with herbs or nasturtiums could brighten up the exterior. If your garden buildings are too prominently positioned, let your head go and plant scented evergreen climbers that will quickly camouflage and add charm. Perhaps an evergreen base of *Ampelopsis sempervirens* draped with a fragrant *Wisteria sinensis*. There is no shed that cannot be beautified with the wonderfully fragrant cupped pink flowers of the rose, Constance Spry. Perhaps you've always wanted somewhere to grow that winter flowering clematis, *Clematis cirrhosa* var. *balaarica*, or somewhere sheltered to grow a lemon tree. However, if the shed is constantly in use, refrain from planting a thorny climber as camouflage!

A working country property may have dog kennels, poultry sheds, garages, meat house, fuel bowser and workshop in close proximity to the garden. If these add to the atmosphere of the surrounding garden and property, they should not be hidden from view. However, if they are tackily built or too practical to be an object of beauty, screening trees or shrubs need to be planted to block them from view.

In one country garden I know, a very simple farm building that was not being used was brought into the garden, surrounded by a verandah and transformed into a charming cottage, totally in keeping with the homestead. It became a focal point for a charming quadrangle enclosed by masses of roses.

A trellis is wonderful for camouflaging unsightly buildings and for those willing to try their hand at a bit of espalier work, training a grape vine, fruit tree or rose along the trellis adds an innovative touch to the garden. An ugly shed may be given a facelift by erecting a simple wooden pergola from old tree limbs and draping it with grape, wisteria or roses. This will soften the structure immeasurably.

Gertrude Jekyll devoted an entire chapter to 'converting ugliness to beauty' in one of her books. 'No plant is more helpful and accommodating than the Rose in the way of screening ugliness

and providing living curtains of flowery drapery for putting over dull and unsightly places.' She suggests using dead trees or any rough branching wood to provide the framework for rustic arbours that are to be clothed with roses. 'What a splendid exercise it would be if people would only go round their places and look for all the ugly corners, and just think how they might be made beautiful by the use of free-growing Roses.'

One of the most accommodating roses I know is Mme Alfred Carriere with its pale, sweetly scented cupped blooms, evergreen

ABOVE: Much of the charm of this farm building is the wonderful colour, which although bright, is delightful in its provincial setting.

OPPOSITE: Wandering from the garden to the outbuildings is an alluring way to explore the country garden. Old machinery sheds (top) or stables (below) add much to the garden's charm.

foliage and almost thornless branches. It is fast growing, constantly in flower and virtually disease resistant. A favourite of Vita Sackville-West, it covered the South Cottage at Sissinghurst. Whenever choosing a rose for growing near a door or walkway, don't be tempted to choose one that grabs at people walking

ABOVE: Away from the mainstream of the garden, this quaint old outbuilding with its pile of wood and patch of rhubarb, has rural appeal.
OPPOSITE: Mellowed stonework is a wonderful backdrop in the rambling, informal style of country garden where old buildings may be used for climbing vines or roses.

past. To be continually pricked by an errant branch is irritating, however charming the rose may be. Mme Legras de St Germain is another near thornless shrub with attractive white flowers, quartered with a green button eye. They flower profusely and may be planted in semi-shade.

Propogating sheds or greenhouses are one of the most practical yet unsightly garden structures. To be effective, they cannot be camouflaged with greenery, so it is best to keep these to the working garden. This working area can be partitioned off by rows of berries, grapes on trellis or fruiting hedges.

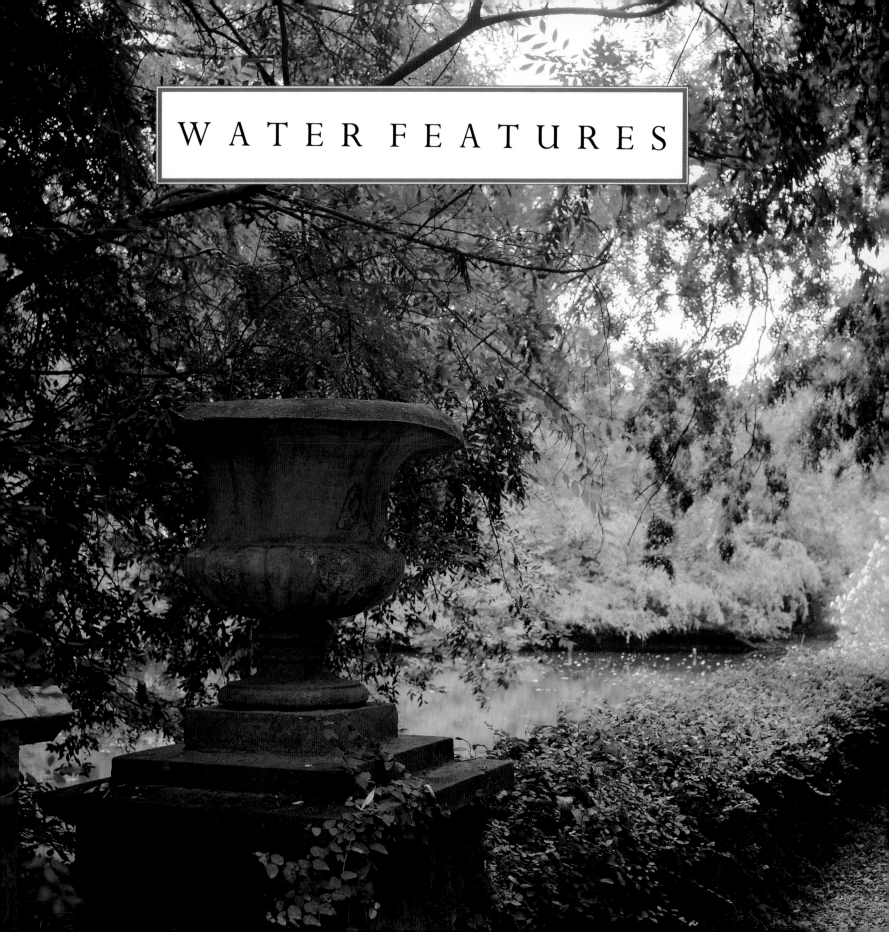

WATER FEATURES

There is no better setting for large expanses of water than in the natural surrounds of the country garden. The many moods water brings into the garden is unmatched by any other garden feature. The tranquillity and peace of still water invites reflection and mirrors the changing skies, while moving water brings a refreshing quality.

Just the mere glimpse of water is compelling, drawing the eye and providing that added dimension. Those lucky enough to have a natural water feature running through or along the edge of the garden, have one of the greatest assets available to the garden designer. How then, to incorporate such a feature into the scheme of the garden? I am in total accord with John Brookes, who writes on the temptation to exploit such natural beauty. Such a step, he writes, can be a mistake, emphasising the man-made feel of the additions and 'the alien decoration will take the edge off the natural charm of the original'.

Sensitively performed, the charm of a small creek may be heightened by the construction of a stone weir or a simple unpainted wooden footbridge. Anything too conspicuous may draw undue attention to itself, thus spoiling the serenity of the garden. As water has a soothing effect on the senses, any man-made additions need to be down-played rather than attention-grabbing.

Throughout the ages, water has played a central role in garden design. There are records dating back to at least 2000 BC, noting that however utilitarian gardens were in the Old Kingdom, formal water pools were incorporated. Mesopotamian courtyards invariably contained water features and later, in Rome, the Emperor Hadrian encouraged expansive stretches of water. There is perhaps no greater example of a lavish use of water from the Middle Ages than at Villa d'Este in Italy, with its majestic terraces and multitude of fountains.

Since earliest times, water was used formally in garden design and it was not until the 1700's that William Kent freed garden design from the long tradition of formality, incorporating natural water features much as we use them today. Lancelot 'Capability' Brown further informalised garden design, and in his quest to sweep away formality in favour of broader landscapes, he

ABOVE: This long narrow stretch of water is glimpsed through a tall clipped cypress hedge that surrounds the classic Roman pool.
OPPOSITE: The Italian urn atop this stone balustrade separates a large lily pond from the entrance driveway that leads into this historic garden.

ABOVE: A glimpse of water in the garden provides tranquility that is hard to emulate with any other medium.

LEFT: Alchemilla mollis *thrives at the edge of this lily pond.*

OPPOSITE ABOVE: The perfect addition to any country garden—a lake and rowing boat.

OPPOSITE BELOW: Large expanses of water are a wonderful asset to the country garden, mirroring the changing seasons and providing a natural link between the garden and countryside beyond.

submerged canals and cascades under expansive lakes. This natural use of water is the one most favoured by country gardeners today, although usually on a far more diminutive scale.

Where there are no natural water features to include in the garden scheme, any man-made scheme needs careful siting. It is most important to place any large expanse of water, such as a pond or lake, at the lowest point of the garden to simulate reality. Natural planting patterns best complement informal drifts of water. John Brookes warns against waterside planting looking like a perennial flower border; he favours growing single types of plant in bold masses. Consideration should be afforded to not only the lower growing lilies and rushes, but also to an upper canopy that will cast reflections and dappled shade.

Matching the type of water feature to the style of garden is paramount. A native garden is best complemented by an informal bush rock pool, while a formal lily pond may be best located in a courtyard area or near the house. Deciding whether to stock the pool with fish or to keep it solely for growing water-loving plants will decide the depth. A shallow pool is not suited to fish due to the build up of algae. A stepped pool is needed to suit both plants and fish. However, while water-lilies prefer still water, some fish must have movement in the water so the pool must have both.

Polythene plastic has made the construction of pools far more achievable by the owner-gardener. Reinforced P.V.C. can be stretched into most shapes with the weight of the water stretching the lining into place. When calculating measurements, allow enough to lap over the top edge. This may then be topped with boulders or pavers and softened with plants.

Trees at the water's edge are wonderful for casting reflections and enhance the play of sunshine on water. Shafts of sunlight on to water add sparkle and verve to a garden whereas pools sited in total shade tend to be gloomy. Pools surrounded by prolific plant growth may lose the continuously changing reflections of sky, clouds, sun and surrounding foliage.

Those gardens without any water feature may use simple birdbaths, troughs, old pumps or water butts to add a glimmer to the garden and attract birdlife. Slabs of rock may be hollowed out with hammer and chisel to make natural looking pools for birds. Inverted or hollowed-out boulders may sometimes be found in the bush or around gold digging areas. These need to be placed beneath trees and shrubs and continually topped up with water. Birds are naturally attracted to water, particularly the honeyeaters, who love bathing, whatever the weather. A quiet sheltered area is most conducive to attracting birds, but it is important to elevate the bird bath if there are cats in the garden.

LEFT: A glimpse of water is seen through a haze of honesty, foxgloves, forget-me-nots and shasta daisies.

OPPOSITE: Nepeta, snow-in-summer and roses bloom in true cottage abundance.

COTTAGE STYLE

There is an unpretentious simplicity in the cottage style of planting that is especially suited to the lifestyle of many country gardeners. The size of the country garden is usually such that, unless there are garden helpers to hand, simplicity is the key. The cottage style gardener is happy to fill the house with flowers and be surrounded by a tapestry of colour with little pretence to colour co-ordination and design.

The modesty and lack of artifice associated with the cottage garden style relies on using simple old-fashioned plants rather than the many dazzling new hybrids. Hardy, fragrant plants are grown in profusion, chosen for their blooms rather than their foliage. There is a happy jumble of flowers of all shapes, colours and sizes with flowers allowed to self-seed at will.

This style of garden ideally suits those with a busy lifestyle, or someone who does not want to be tied to the garden. Its low maintenance aspect means precious hours are not spent on

endless garden chores. Chipping and raking paths, mowing the lawn and cutting back after flowering are the basic requirements and these tasks may be carried out by someone without any horticultural knowledge. This lack of obligation engenders a relaxed appreciation of owning a garden.

Much of the appeal lies in the garden's intimacy. Without the wide open spaces of the typical country garden, there is a series of garden rooms with fences draped in roses, honeysuckle

ABOVE: Old-fashioned climbing roses, such as this Silver Moon rose, invoke a cottage feel to even the grandest of gardens.

OPPOSITE: Valerian is coming back into favour as a mainstay of the country garden, with its hardiness and prolific flowering habit.

and wisteria and seats or benches thoughtfully placed to view and enjoy the garden. A tranquil aura envelops the garden as though nature, not man, were the gardener. Paths flanked with sweet smelling ground covers ramble through the tangle of greenery and flowers. There is a modest, unassuming air of understated beauty.

By strict definition, cottage gardens are those associated with a small dwelling, but in modern terms, it has become a style of gardening more suited to the busy owners of large country gardens or 'weekend gardeners'. Within this style of gardening there are those that favour the romantic; others prefer a wilder look; some use only native plants; others elect to use exotics. Whatever the style, the effect can only be enhanced by keeping to the simple straight species with their dainty blossom and sweet scent, rather than using the showy new hybrids.

Margery Fish, cottage garden advocate, says the plants used in this style of gardening are quite ordinary, with the mainstays being white lilies, clove-scented pinks, honeysuckle, mignonette, roses, primroses, lavender, hollyhocks, hawthorn and amaranthus. Additions to this include rosemary and southernwood, daisies, daffodils, columbines, true geraniums, astrantias and pelargoniums, some grown in pots at the back door.

Traditionally herbs and vegetables were grown in the cottage garden, adding interest and productivity. Among the most beautiful of flowers, herbs greatly add to the charm of the garden bed. Bergamot, lemon balm, borage, lavender, rosemary, garlic chives, dill, fennel, sage, marjoram, thyme, chamomile, angelica, and yarrow are attractive plants in their own right; and their scent and profusion of greenery will enhance any cottage garden scheme. Growing vegetables amongst the greenery is not always successful for optimum culinary results. The lettuce tend to be swamped by the more exuberant flowers and carrots are easy to lose in the mass of greenery. However, edging the vegetable garden with cottage plants adds colour and interest to the more productive area of the garden. Berries are a favourite of cottage style gardeners—gooseberries make wonderful hedges and strawberries are good for edging paths. Mulberries are wonderful to eat straight from the tree and raspberries are delicious fresh.

The cottage style gardener is more likely to opt for productive trees as shelter in the garden. A spreading walnut or plum tree provides a wonderful canopy of shade for table and chairs with the added bonus of fruit or nuts. A cherry walk is ethereally beautiful in summer with its simple white blossom. Quince and apple blossom are among the most beautiful of spring flowers, and medlars, pomegranate and persimmon provide wonderful autumn foliage and unusual fruit for the pantry.

ABOVE: Rosa laevigata *is a robust evergreen rose with startling white single blooms appearing in late spring.*
OPPOSITE: *Cottage favourites: Snow-in-summer, thyme, clematis, poppies and roses provide a tranquil courtyard atmosphere.*

THE WILD GARDEN

ABOVE: *Plants, such as this colourful oxalis, are given their freedom in the wild garden. Simple plants are favoured over rare species and are planted* en masse. OPPOSITE: *That wonderful exponent of the wild garden, William Robinson said of the wild garden that 'the owner might go away for ten years and find it more beautiful than ever on his return'. This is not a garden for the fastidious. Leaves are encouraged to carpet the ground, providing a rich mulch.*

There is no finer environment for the wild style of gardening to be implemented to the full than in the larger expanses of the country garden. The total unpretentiousness of wild gardening lends a certain intrigue and candour that appeals to the psyche of the more romantic gardener. It is not really the *laissez faire* approach so much that appeals, but the very essence of the

wild garden: a subtle, yet unrestrained and uninhibited beauty. To many, this is the garden of fairy tales and childhood books, of dreams and fantasies.

The relaxed informality of wild gardening is more natural and achievable than studied formality. Self-seeding is encouraged and any weeds that do emerge through the mass of greenery are not frowned upon. Simple plants are grown in abundance rather than single specimen plants, which have no place in the wild garden.

ABOVE: The charm of fritillaries is unparalleled in the wild garden where they look wonderful flowering amongst grass. Fritillaries thrive in semi-shaded conditions.
OPPOSITE: Nothing too contrived for the wild garden—furniture needs to look as though it has always been there, as does this charming painted bench, nestled amongst the freesias and natural grass.

ABOVE: A rustic wooden bridge spans the lily pond in this wonderfully wild garden.

OPPOSITE: A child's delight, with leaves to trample in and a swing to play on.

Colour is subtle, and green, in all its hues and textures, predominates. This sensitive use of colour imbues a quiet restfulness and timelessness that is soothing to the nerves, and it is in this part of the garden that the garden owner is most likely to sit and soliloquise.

Traditionally, the wild garden has been one part of the entire garden, an area where nature is allowed to play its hand; an area to balance the more structured areas. Here, design is simple, creating a feeling of enclosure with sweeping curves and broad brush strokes of bulbs and groundcovers. Greater effect is achieved by repeating planting themes—planting masses of one type of tree, shrub or groundcover.

There should be a sense of mystery and an allure that draws one into the heart of the wild garden, with paths wandering off to who knows where. A leafy opening amongst a thicket of trees or old iron gate may herald the entrance to the wild area. Nothing too contrived or *new*! Freshly painted white gates would look too glaringly obvious and detract from the feeling of peace and harmony.

Sculpture, if used at all, must be subtle in the extreme. Far more pleasure is gained from glimpsing a discreet piece of muted statuary nestling down amongst the greenery than one that immediately demands attention. Nothing should dominate in the wild garden. The utter simplicity and restfulness will provide beauty enough. Seating invites reflection and needs to be in keeping with the setting—nothing too ornate.

Plant selection is totally to the gardener's liking. Many prefer to use only indigenous plants in a natural setting. In Australia, the beauty of the native flora is extensive and unique; with its broad canvas of eucalypts with their wonderful textured trunks, subtle blossom and bark; bird-attracting grevilleas, callistemon, banksia and waratah; and carpets of everlasting daisies. There is also a tremendous variety of native flora, with more than 600 species of eucalypts alone.

Older gardens, whether established with exotic or native plants, have an atmosphere of their own. A wild garden created afresh, while enjoying an overall plan using particular plants and trees, lacks the atmosphere of a garden created amongst mature trees. If there is water in the form of a stream, creek or river anywhere in the vicinity of the garden, incorporating this into the perimeter of the wild garden will add much to its allure.

LEFT: A sense of mystery and allure draws the visitor into the wild garden.
OPPOSITE: Poppies naturalised in an orchard of olive trees.
FOLLOWING PAGES: Hedges provide a strong architectural framework that carries the garden through the stripped back winter months.

SYMMETRY AND PERSPECTIVE

Formal axes and vistas of many of the great gardens of centuries past are usually on too grand a scale to equate to country gardens today. However, this linear concept may be redefined and adapted on a far more modest scale.

PATTERNS AND VISTAS

Such is the scale of the rural landscape that vistas may be augmented in country gardens to enhance a particular feature of the garden or a faraway scene. Distant points of interest are brought into perspective when viewed along a vista, rather than seen in a sweeping panoramic scene.

Formal axes and vistas of many of the great gardens of centuries past, while stunning to view, are usually on too grand a scale to equate to country gardens today. However, this linear concept may be redefined and adapted on a far more modest scale by simple plant selection and paving material. A rustic farm gate at the end of a long gravel path; an allee of fruit trees framing a distant view; or a tree lined driveway has great appeal in a rural setting.

The formal symmetry of a straight walkway may be neutralised by abundant growth, with plants spilling onto the path, softening the line. An architectural framework of paths, walls and steps may be played down to a great extent when clothed with a mantle of greenery. Such a framework may be the making of a garden, serving as the skeleton of the overall design, providing the 'bones' in the less exuberant winter months. Hedges also provide a strong structural statement—either formal clipped hedges or more romantic tapestry hedging.

ABOVE: This wonderful long staircase is flanked by clipped Yew hedging, with aubretias flowering in the foreground.

LEFT: Distant vistas may be accentuated by leaving areas open or removing mature trees and creating a point of interest with the use of sculpture.

OPPOSITE: This parterre is far beyond the realms of most country gardens, but demonstrates the strength of design in using clipped hedging, even if it is only as a border or background within the garden.

Symmetrical landscaping is pleasing to the eye, with plantings mirrored on a central axis. However, much rural architecture is distinctly asymmetrical, calling for a less formal garden layout. Although I tend towards slight dishevelment in my choice of gardens, I still favour a strong architectural layout, with straight paths and axes, and vistas to draw the eye. Such gardens are a joy to photograph and undoubtedly have greater strength in winter, when foliage doesn't camouflage flaws.

The great test of a garden is to hold its own during the colder months of the year when the garden is not *en fête*. While most gardens look after themselves in spring, this is but a brief interval in the gardening year. Incorporating patterns and vistas greatly strengthen a garden, providing a pleasing sense of structure. Blooms and foliage then become the means of filling in the picture rather than the sole means for the garden's existence.

ABOVE: Knot gardens depend to a great extent on the contrast in foliage between the hedging and the plants grown within the borders. Here, clipped box contain plantings of lavender with the sundial providing a focal point.
LEFT: Evergreen hedging and symmetrical design along a central axis add much to the exploration of the garden in winter.
OPPOSITE: Fragrant garden walks are far more evocative than those without any semblance of aroma. Wisteria is a favourite for its fragrance, beauty and shade.

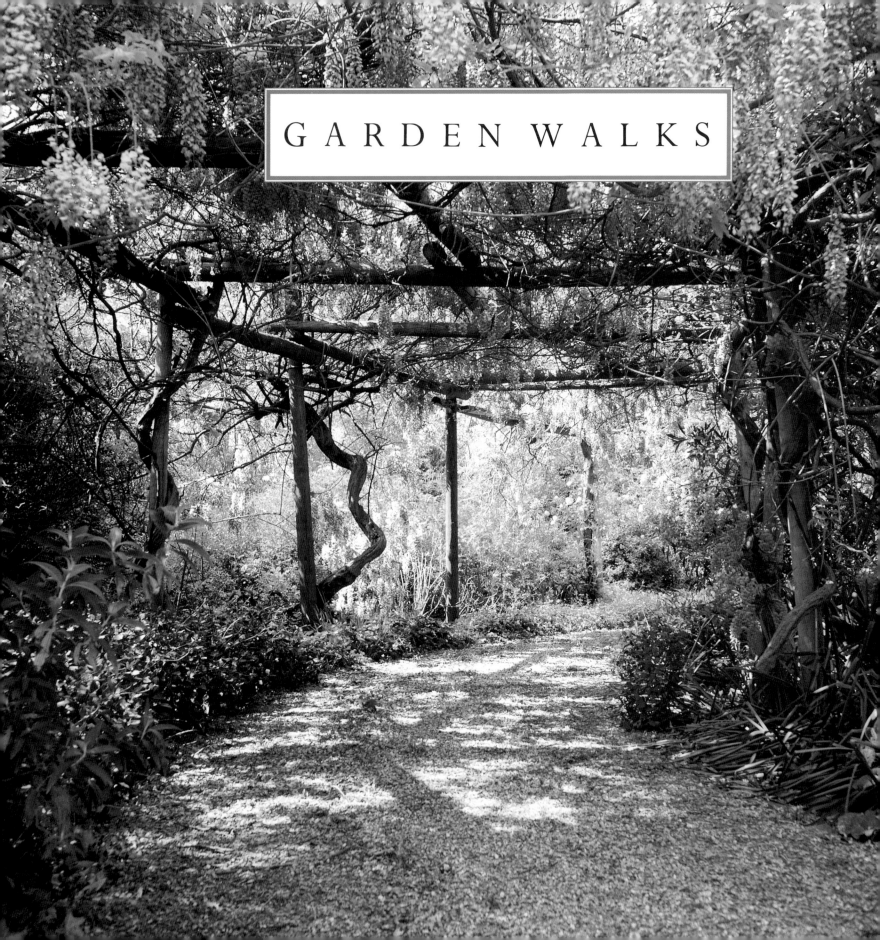

GARDEN WALKS

ABOVE: A very traditional cottage path, flanked with Queen Anne's Lace, geraniums and silene.

ABOVE RIGHT: An informal stone paved path is made more appealing by the little Bellis perennis *daisies that have self seeded and flower with great abandon.*

Paths and walkways are one of the most effective ways of romanticising or individualising a garden. Enticing paths leading through the greenery to secluded corners lend an intimate aura to any garden. To see the entire garden in one sweep is disappointing. Creating garden rooms linked by walks introduces an illusion of space, adding much to the allure of the garden.

Paths lend substance to a garden, inviting exploration into the far reaches of the shrubberies. They beckon and lure the garden visitor to secluded corners. They also take out the indecision of where to start exploring the garden. Vast expanses of lawn are appealing to look at, but do not necessarily invite closer inspection of the garden borders.

When creating paths, it is important to identify the most used traffic area. Many garden owners say they wait to see where most of the traffic is before creating a pathway. It is pointless to create an alluring pathway that no-one uses, when it is simply far quicker to tramp across a few bulbs to reach the same destination. The human foible of taking the shortest possible distance between any two areas is accentuated in wet or inclement

weather. Weighing up practicality with pure aesthetics, paths need to look part of the garden without being too obvious and dominating the entire scene.

More importantly, paths need to actually lead somewhere. How disappointing to wander along a path that abruptly ends and you are left to retrace your steps along the self-same path. What these paths lack is a sense of purpose—perhaps a garden bench, a small pond, a piece of sculpture or a distant vista would provide a good enough reason to wander through that particular part of the garden.

The width of walkways is dictated by the surrounding plant growth—the narrower and more intimate, the more mysterious. However, it can be disconcerting to have to battle with a jungle of greenery and duck under low branches to move from one part of the garden to another, particularly when the foliage is damp and heavy with water. Entrance paths need to be wide enough to enable at least two people to walk along comfortably.

Christopher Lloyd writes that one of the greatest pleasures of gardening is to walk about the garden with a friend, looking at and discussing the plants. As this is essentially the purpose of a path—a means of exploring the garden—the surface needs

ABOVE: Ideally, paths need to lead somewhere specific, and a gate left ajar at the end of a path is great enticement to wander further.

ABOVE LEFT: This immaculately kept path, edged on one side with clipped box and on the other with neat stone edging, winds through the most interesting parts of the garden.

LEFT: The cottage garden path is usually gravel, narrow, flanked with masses of perennials, in this case, pinks, lavenders, snow-in-summer and roses. The elegant archway is planted with the Noisette, Alister Stella Gray, a fragrant golden rambler.
OPPOSITE: Christopher Lloyd writes that one of the greatest pleasures of gardening is to walk about the garden with a friend, looking at and discussing the plants. This is essentially the primary purpose of a path—a means of exploring the garden. Gravel paths have a natural look and in this garden are bordered with old terracotta tiles made on the property.

to be stable and smooth enough so that there is no hazard in negotiation. Irregularly placed paving may be disconcerting, averting the eyes from the garden to watch one's step!

Grass walkways are pleasing in the overall visage of the garden, creating a vision of harmony. There is something restful and elegant in green walkways of lawn between garden borders. Alternatively, stepping stones placed in the lawn lead the eye onwards and provide a stable surface for walkers. Gravel is a traditional and natural-looking medium for country garden paths and is given an instant facelift by an occasional raking. Borders spilling onto the path lend a more casual air, while hedging is a more classical edging alternative.

Walkways may be lined with lavender or thyme for a scented cottage look; with helleborus in a shady area; with clipped *buxus* for a more formal effect; with violets or lawn daisies in a wild garden; or rows of parsley or chives in the kitchen garden. In an informal garden, a juxtaposition of colours, scents and varieties of plants spilling onto a gravel or flagged stone path create pockets of interest and a reason to pause on garden walks.

Paths and walkways are also used for creating lines of an axis and for drawing the eye to distant viewpoints. They provide an architectural element that becomes a strong part of the garden's overall design. Moreover, they dictate the angle from which the garden is viewed—a vital consideration.

AVENUES

The relaxed informality of the country garden is the ideal setting for an understated avenue of trees or shrubs. However simple, such a feature will give immense strength and structure to a garden, imparting an architectural framework that stands on its own throughout the seasonal changes.

Connotations of grandeur have led to a diminishing use of this strongly architectural statement in many countries. However, far from being purely decorative, they provide valuable wind shelter and shade, so often needed in windswept rural areas. The scale, style and choice of plants will also fashion their impact, perhaps lessening their traditional grandeur.

The one static feature of the avenue, however informally planted, is its even and regular appearance. To ensure this, similarly sized plants should be placed at regular intervals and will then hopefully grow at an even rate. There are no rules

ABOVE: Vistas may be accentuated with the use of arbours.

ABOVE LEFT: Avenues planted with the one type of tree have far greater visual impact than a tapestry effect. This driveway of elms is impressive throughout the seasons.

OPPOSITE: This avenue of stately chestnuts has both a decorative and structural role in this large garden.

LEFT: Trident Maples have been pleached to form an allee as one of the main entrances into this large country garden.
OPPOSITE: There is great anticipation on reaching the destination when approaching a garden through a thicket of greenery.

for planting distances as this entirely depends on the species of plant chosen. Trees with a large spreading canopy will obviously need far more space than fastigiate (tapering) trees. Double rows may strengthen the impact of the avenue.

The telescopic illusion is heightened by drawing the eye through the avenue to a definite object. A building, water feature, sculpture or seat leads the eye onwards and invites exploration. Pollarding or pleaching the trees formalises the concept while selecting plants of different species creates a more informal, tapestry effect.

Avenues need not be straight—in fact there is a greater sense of anticipation in a curved avenue. Humphrey Repton (1752-1818), a leading English landscape architect of his time, wrote of the virtue of an avenue 'that climbs up a hill and, passing over the summit, leaves the fancy to conceive its determination'. Another eighteenth century designer, William Kent, informalised the concept by clumping together groups at irregular intervals, permitting views from the central axis to the countryside beyond. The French style of the seventeenth century was to cut a swathe through natural forest to create a feeling of distance and to

focus the onlooker's eye to some distant point.

In the more relaxed style of gardening adopted by country gardeners today, these concepts may still be carried out in a far more informal mode. In Australia, the local eucalypts with their magnificent trunks and towering canopies have been utilised to full effect in informal plantings, particularly where there are glimpses through the avenue to the natural bushland beyond.

The traditional avenue plantings of *Tilia cordata*, the small-leaved lime; *Aesculus hippocastanum*, horse chestnut; *Fagus sylvatica*, beech; *Platanus* and *Quercus* species are still being planted for

future generations, but for those wanting a faster growing avenue (one they can enjoy in their own lifetime) other species are favoured, including *Pyrus ussuriensis*, the Manchurian Pear; *Populus* species—*tremuloides, canadensis, nigra, deltoides, simonii* and *alba*; *Robinia pseudacacia*, the false acacia; and *Eucalyptus*. Productive fruit and nut trees may also be used with great panache—the walnut being a prime example of a magnificently shaped tree that also bears worthwhile crops of nuts. Avenues of almonds, fig, medlars, quince, pears or whatever thrives in the vicinity may be used to great effect.

HEDGES

Great Dixter (above) is one of the most inspiring gardens to visit, particularly in terms of the enterprising way hedges and topiary have been used. Transposed to the country garden (opposite) hedges provide a strong harmonious boundary or background, and in cool climates, a wonderful framework for the bare winter months.

Hedges are the most versatile of garden structures, providing a harmonious link between garden and countryside. They personalise a garden and provide a wonderful backdrop within the garden.

Hedges serve a number of purposes: they delineate boundaries, provide privacy, act as a barrier to stock or intruders, and may be used as windbreaks. Such 'living fences' are far more in harmony with the rural landscape than man-made

LEFT: One of the basic rules of planting hedges is that plants should be propagated from the same source or be well matched. When establishing a hedge, it is a good idea to put one or two spare plants somewhere in the garden so that if part of the hedge dies, there will be grown plants of the same ilk to replace them with. OPPOSITE: Clipped box hedging provides a disciplined border for the exuberant herbaceous planting behind.

structures, and their richness of texture and foliage can only enhance both garden and surroundings.

More economical than a traditional fence to construct, perhaps their major drawback is that they are not 'instant'. It may take years to achieve the acquired effect. In the country garden, garden boundaries need to be stock- or dog-proof, requiring the construction of a temporary netting fence until the hedge has grown to maturity. A simple method of growing an informal hedge is to use the stock-proof fence as the base for a hedge. Within a year or two there need not be any visible trace of the utilitarian fence as the hedge envelopes the structure.

There are few rules for growing hedges other than avoiding planting too close together, which may result in dead wood if any of the plants die. When choosing a hedge as opposed to a fence, consider the clipping required for formal hedging. Depending on the plant species, this needs to be carried out

once, or maybe twice a year. The upkeep is worth the effect, particularly on small scale hedges used within the garden boundaries. As with mowing the lawn, trimming a hedge gives the garden an instant facelift.

Tapestry hedging is one of the most whimsical and easiest forms of hedging to achieve. All manner of plant material may be used to great effect. An evergreen base such as *Viburnum tinus, Cupressus, Cotoneaster, Escallonia, Abelia, Acacia, Banksia,* *Callistemon, Grevillea, Hakea, Leptospermum, Ficus, Pyracantha, Choisya ternata, Arbutus,* Lilly pilly, laurel, holly, myrtle or olive can be planted with flowering climbers such as honeysuckle, wisteria, roses, jasmine, clematis, *Mandevilla, Pandorea, Sollya heterophylla, Parthenocissus, Solanum jasminoides* or grape. Year round interest may be achieved by including autumn colouring shrubs or climbers and winter berry-bearing shrubs.

A grey foliage hedge has particular appeal where the farm

ABOVE: The soft cream flowers of the Photinia *makes this a popular choice for a more informal hedge.*

ABOVE RIGHT: This informal Spinosissima *rose hedge is wonderfully fragrant when in bloom during late spring.*

OPPOSITE: Hedging may be used, as in this entrance, to conceal the garden beyond.

buildings have a slate or charcoal coloured roof. Such hedges look wonderful in winter against the grey trunks of trees and deciduous shrubs. *Teucrium fruticans* is a hardy evergreen shrub with pale china blue flowers against pale grey foliage, which makes a soft looking hedge growing to 2.5 metres. French or English lavender make a wonderfully romantic hedge with its mantle of mauve flowers throughout summer. Santolina makes an attractive low hedge and is best kept clipped. Westringia and rosemary are an attractive year round formal clipped hedge. *Buddleias* could be used for a taller growing hedge while many of the Australian native grevillea, callistemon or banksia may be selected for their grey foliage and to encourage birds into the garden.

A novel approach is to use edible plants for hedging. This can be particularly effective in screening the kitchen garden from the prevailing wind or in less formal areas of the garden. A gooseberry hedge makes an attractive stock-proof formal hedge similar to a *Rosa mundi* or sweet briar hedge. Thornless edible hedges can be planted using dwarf citrus, elderberry or carob. Unclipped hedges will yield less fruit than those that are clipped. Some varieties to select from are avocado, blueberry, currant,

pomegranate or any of the dwarf fruiting trees. Quince, pear, peach, apricot, apple and plum will make taller hedges. These will not fruit to full capacity but will look wonderful, particularly when laden with fruit.

In an old-fashioned country garden, a may or Persian lilac hedge lends a nostalgic air. Clipped *Buxus* or *Lonicera nitida* provide an evergreen backdrop to a more formal area of the garden. Traditionally roses have been used for hedging through the ages and there are many that lend themselves to a country garden hedge: the old-fashioned striped *Rosa mundi* for a clipped formal hedge; the delicate pink, sweetly scented Stanwell Perpetual for a low informal hedge; Complicata with its brilliant single pink blooms for a larger, more informal hedge; the white rugosa, Schneezwerg, with its perpetual flowering habit and coloured helps; Kathleen Harrop for a thornless hedge of perpetual flowering, fragrant, pale pink roses; the floriferous pink flowering Meidiland Bonica; or David Austin rose hedge. Some of the thorny evergreen climbing or rambling roses, such as Mermaid,

Silver Moon, Wedding Day, *Rosa filipes* 'Kiftsgate', *Rosa gigantea, Rosa laevigata* or *Rosa bracteata* make wonderful dense flowering, informal stock-proof hedges over existing fences. Thornless (or near thornless) roses such as the banksias, Madame Alfred Carriere or Cecile Brunner are better choices at gateways.

A japonica hedge (pale apricot, white or red) makes an effective stock and dog-proof barrier and has the added bonus of winter blossom. Many of the species and briar roses serve the same purpose and provide an impenetrable barrier, as do pyracanthas, berberis and natal plums. There is little that can surpass the common hawthorn (*Crataegus monogyna*) as an effective and attractive hedge for the outer perimeters of the country garden. Its abundance of sweetly scented spring blossom is followed by a blaze of red berries. Its simple beauty enthralled even Shakespeare:

Gives not the hawthorn bush a sweeter shade
Than doth a rich embroidered canopy?

COLOUR

In country gardens, where harmony is fostered more than the need to make a visual statement, colour selection is paramount. This is highly personal and needs to come from the heart, not from fashion trends.

THE FLOWER
BORDER

ABOVE: A drift of yellow yarrow, Achillea filipendulina, *is brilliant in its intensity and highlights the summer border.*

OPPOSITE: Creating a pleasing herbaceous border is perhaps one of the most exacting tasks in the garden. It is not a matter of simply having everything flowering in one grand sweep, but how they perform together throughout the year.

PREVIOUS PAGES: Although both have striking colours, the rich green background brings harmony to this planting scheme of scarlet foxgloves and brilliant yellow evening primroses (Oenothera).

Creating a flower border is one of the most exacting of horticultural tasks. To compose a picture using foliage, colour, texture and form where the medium is never static is quite an achievement. To envisage the change from season to season requires a thorough knowledge of the plants to be used: how long they flower for, their height, how they look from season to season, and their colour and form.

The transient beauty of the mixed border creates an ongoing challenge for gardeners. Artistic composition and plant selection

and placement is not something that one suddenly attains; it is a matter of much trial and error, learning from mistakes, moving plants, visiting other gardens and reading garden literature.

Deciding on a colour theme is of foremost importance. If soft colours are the theme, the glaring orange of the marigold or oriental poppy may be out of place. If red flowering plants are chosen, they may conflict with the pinks, yet look stunning against blue blooms. Yellows and blues are a pleasing combination, as are purple and pinks. Cream and white coloured flowers will offset any colour combination. To complete the tapestry, all shades of green are woven through, highlighting and complementing the chosen hues.

Bright colours look wonderful against a dark backdrop of green, be it hedge, wall or lawn. In a dry garden where there is not enough water to keep the lawn green, muted colours and abundant greenery take away the harshness. Pale colours

are easier to use effectively and do not distract the eye as much as brilliant hues. Cool colours, such as green, blue, yellow and white have a soothing influence; green being the most restful colour. An area devoted entirely to green foliage is particularly effective. Many flowers are tinged with green, such as *Alchemilla erythropoda* or *alpina* (Lady's Mantle) with soft green flowers; *Helleborus foetidus, Geum, Rivale album, Polygonatum falcatum* (Japanese Solomon's Seal), *Nicotiana alata, Amaranthus caudatus, Kochia scoparia, Viola hederacea, Grevillea citriodora* and Green Ice rose.

Colours vary with the intensity of sunlight and shade. Bright colours planted in shade lose their strength just as cool, luminous colours glow in shady positions. The soft green foliage and white flowers of *Campanula latifolia alba, Campanula persicifolia alba, Campanula latiloba alba, Anenome sylvestris, Anenome vitifolia, Anenome nemorosa, Anenome canadensis* or *Digitalis purpurea* will brighten shady areas.

ABOVE: An informal planting of foxgloves, valerian, forget-me-nots and daisies provides a pleasing combination.

OPPOSITE (ABOVE): Many gardeners use their flower borders as an artist uses a canvas, implementing the hues and colours that appeal.

OPPOSITE (BELOW): Colour preference in the garden is often dictated by outside influences, such as the colour of the roof or walls of the house. In this instance, the muted colour of the house is complemented by the pastel tonings of the foxgloves and aquilegias.

In country gardens, where harmony is fostered more than the need to make a visual statement, colour selection is paramount. This is highly personal and needs to come from the heart, not from fashion trends. What is jarring to someone, need not be to another. To create your own individual garden, use the flower border as an artist's palette, implementing the hues and colour combinations that appeal to your own sense of style. Personal

ABOVE: Red is perhaps one of the hardest colours to place in the flower border, but here, the brilliant tonings of the bergamot, Monarda didyma, are complemented by the pure white blooms of the Californian poppy, Romneya coulteri.

OPPOSITE: There is an art in using bright colours in the garden and many gardeners are hesitant when using primary colours such as yellow, red and blue together. However the effect may be stunning, particularly if there is a predominance of green, such as this ancient yew hedge in the background.

style is innate to each individual. When visiting gardens or looking through books, there are some 'garden pictures' that instantly appeal. Try to analyse this appeal—is it the colours, the design, the shape of a plant or a combination of all these?

Russell Page advocates choosing a theme, enhancing it in every way possible and then eliminating distracting details. If the theme is a colour combination, such as blue and white,

be ruthless with any straying colour as this will focus the eye on one particular plant rather than endow a feeling of total harmony.

Knowledge of flowering periods is vital. A blue and white border may end up monochrome if the flowering of both blue and white plants does not coincide. As spring is the peak flowering time, a spring border is an easier task to create than a border

in full flower mid-summer. If summer is the time the family spends in the garden, try for a summer display. Do not, however, ignore the stripped back winter look. If the border is totally dormant for six months of the year, choose plants that provide some greenery in winter—particularly along a front entrance or in beds bordering the house. While some advocate a total splash in one orchestrated sweep, I would rather have something of interest in every part of the garden during every season of the year. It is a great delight to wander in the garden and stumble upon an unexpected bloom or waft of scent.

Monet was one of the greatest exponents of unabashedly using colour in the borders. His garden at Giverny is saturated with colour, endearing even the purist to Monet's extravagant combinations of colours. He planned his garden as he painted his canvases—with great splashes of rich hues. The lush plantings with not a speck of soil showing and informal groupings of plants is in true country garden style, albeit with a French flavour.

Overall harmony is important. Colours need to blend in with the background. It is pointless keeping red out of the planting scheme if the roof of your house is painted red. Similarly, if the walls of the house are bagged with terracotta, greens and creams will complement the building, but rose pink would look out of place. Grey foliage plants look wonderful against a house with a grey painted or slate tiled roof.

Most people have strong colour preferences and their choice is reflected in their garden, their houses and their clothes. Colour schemes within a house, particularly rooms with large windows, may to a certain extent dictate the colours used in the surrounding garden. A yellow sunroom may be complemented by a number of yellow plants in the garden beyond, and a mauve bedroom could have lilac wisteria garlanding the window.

ABOVE LEFT: In this garden, a wonderfully constructed dry stone wall provides a strong background to the cottage style planting.

LEFT: The striking bluish-purple spires of Echium fastuosum *and* Campanula latifolia *look stunning together, highlighted by the late afternoon sun.*

OPPOSITE: Planning a border requires thorough knowledge of plant types. Flowering is not the only factor—shape, foliage and height are important. This spring flowering of forget-me-nots, aquilegias, azaleas, and Bellis perennis *is a pleasing combination.*

PLANNING
THE BORDER

Rich soil is the key to a successful border. Organic matter, compost, peat and manure should be dug in before planting. The actual planting may be in the mind's eye, but even so, notes and sketches are helpful. For the more methodical, the border may be drawn in scale with the dimensions of plants pencilled in. Plants need to overlap so there is no soil showing. Dainty plants should be kept away from more invasive ones, while evergreen plants need to be interspersed with herbaceous plants which die back or disappear for long periods. *Paeonia* and lilies, which hibernate in winter, need to be underplanted with small bulbs for early spring flowering to prevent large bare patches in the border.

A comprehensive gardening diary or card catalogue is needed for the keen gardener, noting plant development and movements. Those plants that have a total winter dormancy need some record kept of when they reappear. Note when the plant starts and stops flowering. This makes the task of planning so much easier. A plan or good memory is needed to stop newly established dainty plants being overtaken by self-seeding annuals such as poppies, cosmos, love-in-a-mist or tobacco plant. These tend to totally swamp everything in their way.

Planning a border for year round interest may require subtle planting associations. Bulbs, shrubs, annuals and perennials may all be used for an extended season. The border need not necessarily be solely herbaceous or perennial. In the relaxed atmosphere of the country garden, a mixed border has prolonged appeal.

Flowering periods are not the only consideration in planning the border. Shape is essential. Interest is created by using differing heights—spires of delphiniums set off lower growing clumps of cranesbill or *Helleborus*. The bold foliage of *Acanthus* with its tall summer spires may contrast with the drooping heads of *Polygonatum multiflorum* (Solomon's seal).

LEFT: This border of Digitalis, Alchemilla *and iris is in pleasant and colourful contrast to the plain brick wall beyond.*

OPPOSITE: A wonderfully exuberant flower border in late spring, full of life and colour.

While it is important not to waste space with mediocre plants, there are those that while not a highlight of the garden or even considered worthy of picking for flower arrangements, provide much needed 'fill in'. A plant that springs to mind in this category is the white valerian (*Centranthus*) with its feathery white flower heads—a good 'fill in' throughout the summer.

Choosing plants on their merits means taking into consideration the length of their flowering period. Some plants, such as poppies and lilies, do not flower for long, but do so with a flourish. Choose the mainstays of the border carefully. Among the long-flowering perennials are *Achillea, Allium, Althaea, Anemone, Anthemis, Aquilegia, Bellis perennis, Campanula, Chrysanthemum, Coreopsis, Delphinium, Dianthus, Dicentra, Gaura lindheimeri, Gypsophila, Helichrysum, Linaria, Lychnis, Monarda, Phlox, Salvia* and *Viola*. Flowering will be prolonged with many of these if the flowers are dead-headed regularly.

When planning the border, a three-tiered method shows plants to their greatest advantage, with the low, ground-hugging plants edging the path or lawn, building up to a tall background. Broad-brush planting is effective in the larger sweep of the country garden. Repeated haphazard groupings of the same plant along the border looks stunning from a distance. Similarly mass planting of a small number of species has a wonderful simplicity, providing a season of glory followed by a mass of greenery that is so refreshing in a large expanse. Much of the appeal of the country garden lies in the breadth of scale and simplicity of planting.

ROSES

ABOVE: This hybrid musk, Penelope, is one of the most prolific of roses, flowering from early spring to autumn. It is highly favoured as a hedging rose, and is often grown amongst perennials, as in this garden.

OPPOSITE: Henri Martin is a Damask Moss which grows to 2 metres with semi-double bright scarlet flowers in loose clusters.

Roses have rightfully earned their place as one of the most popular choices for the country garden. Their colour, fragrance, beauty, hardiness and form are virtually unequalled amongst shrubs. Equally at home in the most casual country garden or formal parterre, their charm is undeniable. Their variety is infinite and for those who enjoy the challenge of selecting the not so common varieties, there are thousands of types available; roses

that flower perpetually, those with autumn foliage, some with brightly coloured heps, evergreen varieties, thornless roses, single or double blooms. There are roses for arches, roses for hedges, roses for borders and roses to cover unsightly sheds and fences.

The rose is so versatile and beloved that there would be few country gardens without one. Thankfully, the days are gone when roses were solely relegated to special rose beds. Grown in mixed plantings, they have tremendous charm and are greatly enhanced by herbaceous perennials such as lilies, campanulas, delphiniums, iris, *aquilegia* and *Alchemilla mollis*. They may be grown amongst foxgloves, hollyhocks, love-in-a-mist, honesty, lavender, solomon's seal and poppies for an old-fashioned look. They look ethereal glimpsed through the white froth of *Crambe cordifolia, gypsophila* or *Amni majus* (Queen Anne's Lace). Roses may be underplanted with rue, garlic chives, borage, lavenders and thyme in the herb garden; or edging the kitchen garden; trained over pergolas or arches; espaliered; weeping; climbing; rambling; ground-covering or grown as standards; their versatility is infinite.

The romance of the rose is much of their appeal. Often described as the queen of flowers, their history dates back to ancient times. In museums there are fossil remains of roses millions of years old. The rose was the religious emblem of the Medes and Persians centuries before Christ; the oldest pictures of roses come from Crete in 1600 BC. The Chinese Emperor had 600 books on roses in his library as early as 500 BC. During the Roman Empire, the rose was at the peak of its prominence, both for its medicinal value and as a symbol of extravagance. After the fall of Rome, the rose gradually crept into religious favour and the earliest Catholic beads were carved in the shape of a rose, giving rise to the name Rosary. England's longest civil war—the War of the Roses—is well documented and the rose was chosen as the emblem of many English Kings.

Empress Josephine Bonaparte is an integral figure in the history of the rose. An ardent collector, she acquired roses from throughout the world to grow in her garden at Malmaison. Also interested in developing new varieties, she encouraged her gardeners to hybridise the many roses she had collected. It was

ABOVE: A pleasing plant combination of Acanthus mollis *with the free flowering blush pink rose, Dr W. Van Fleet.*
OPPOSITE: Cottage plants such as campion, lavender, foxgloves and iris are the perfect foil for old-fashioned roses, providing a mass of greenery and blooms.

entirely due to her royal patronage that the rose became fashionable and that Pierre Redoute was commissioned to paint an everlasting record immortalising the rose.

Beauty and history aside, the rose has long been valued for its medicinal properties. The rose petal was associated from ancient times with the healing of tuberculosis and the alleviation of rheumatism. The recuperating power of rose petals was known to Roman ladies and in the Middle Ages rose oil was used for eye complaints. Rose hips are a known source of Vitamin C and are used to help prevent scurvy. The ancient Apothecary's rose, *Rosa gallica officinalis* has been used for soothing headaches and hysteria as well as making cosmetics. Recent research has *proved* the medicinal properties of roses. Roses contain elements

with astringent and anti-inflammatory properties, and oil, wax, tannin and sugar. They are also full of Vitamin C.

The fragrance of the rose has long been treasured, and attar of roses is prized by the perfume industry. It is said to take three million rose blooms to make one pound of attar. Country gardeners, hating waste, are adept at utilising rose petals for pot pourris, vinegars, jams, butters, and rose hips for syrups and jellies. It is a tranquil vocation wandering amongst the roses with secateurs in hand, picking for vases, pot pourris or simply dead-heading—a peaceful way to view the garden.

In recent years there has been a revival of interest in the old roses. Largely forgotten by the masses for years, their revival brings the fragrance and form redolent of years past. The gallicas,

ABOVE: *This delightfully fragrant hybrid rambler, Albertine, produces a stunning display of salmon-pink flowers in midsummer.*

OPPOSITE: *Titian and iceberg roses flowering in profusion.*

cabbage, centifolias, damasks, musks, moss and rugosa roses are as popular today as they were centuries ago, despite the hybridisation that has produced the more floriferous and brightly-coloured newer varieties. The elegant flowers and perpetual blooms of the modern hybrids are not always able to compete with the beauty and old-wordliness of the old roses. The modern roses are also more tender and disease-prone.

A wonderful compromise has been reached with the introduction of the David Austin roses. Through the use of genetics, Austin was able to create rose history. In the early 1960s he successfully crossed a 1845 gallica, Belle Isis, with a 1938 floribunda, Dainty Maid—effectively combining the old with the new. This resulted in the magnificent Constance Spry rose, with its fragrant cupped blooms of purest pink. He has since gone one step further—to produce roses that are 'old-fashioned' in flower and bush coupled with a recurrent flowering

The variety is so infinite, it is well worth the time to study a rose catalogue or book, or visit a rose or Botanic Garden that has named varieties on display. Many gardeners still settle for the familiar varieties while there are so many more unusual, more beautiful roses that are not commonly seen. Gardeners often still choose a Dorothy Perkins or yellow banksia rose for a pergola or arch, when there are far more free flowering, perfumed, attractive roses that would serve the same purpose. Use thornless climbers along verandah posts and over narrow rose arches; evergreen roses to hide unsightly garden sheds, tanks or fences; thorny shrub roses for stock-proof fencing; perpetual or recurrent flowering roses in the front borders; and the species roses in areas where their heps and autumn foliage will be appreciated. Don't be content to settle for the ordinary. If pale pink roses are your interest, look for Souvenir de St Anne's (semi-double shell pink fragrant recurrent blooms), Countess Bertha (double cupped perpetual flowering), Kathleen Harrop (perpetual flowering and thornless), Chaucer (vigorous, strongly scented double blooms) or Stanwell Perpetual (low growing, richly fragrant and perpetual flowering).

Among the yellow roses are Graham Thomas, Mary Webb, Yellow Charles Austin (David Austin roses); Golden Wings, Fruhlingsgold and Fruhlingsanfang (large single shrub-climbers); the large single climbing Mermaid; *Rosa foetida, R. primula, R. sericea f. lutea* and *R. kokanica* (species roses); Ambassador, Dutch Gold, Midas (Hybrid Teas); and Chinatown, English Holiday, and Mountbatten (Floribundas).

White roses are a wonderful foil to any other plant in the garden. Some popular choices are Wedding Day, *Rosa filipes* 'Kiftsgate', Silver Moon, Gigantea, or *Rosa bracteata* (evergreen climbing roses); Madame Hardy, Mme Zoetmans, Botzaris (Damasks); Frau Karl Druschki (said to be one of the greatest white flowers ever raised); and the rugosas *Blanc Double de Coubert, Souvenir de Philemon Cochet, Schneezwerg* and *Rosa rugosa* 'Alba'.

I have come to love the soft russet tones of many of the English roses with their subtle blend of old gold and apricot tonings, coupled with a rich fragrance. Roses like Cressida, Troilus, Leander, Emanuel and English Garden. In the hybrid

ABOVE: The single, cream-yellow blooms of this Bracteata *climber,* Mermaid, *are immense. It is tolerant of a shady position, and is quite disease resistant.*

habit. With all the desirable qualities of the new and old roses, he has successfully created 'new roses in the old tradition'. This was the aim of rose breeders when they created the Hybrid Tea. Some of the most popular of Austin's roses are Heritage, Canterbury, Dame Prudence, The Prioress, Moonbeam, Chaucer, The Yeoman, The Wife of Bath, Graham Thomas and Gertrude Jekyll.

In large country gardens there is a place for many different types of roses. For their hardiness alone, they are a welcome addition to dry cold climate gardens. This hardiness is evident if you wander in old graveyards or abandoned ruins, where roses often grow without watering or pruning, unassisted for decades.

RIGHT: This evergreen rambler, Rosa fortuneana, *has a mass of creamy white double flowers in spring.*

teas, Summer Love, Maid of Honour, Rosemary Harkness and the climbing tea, Lady Hillingdon, have the same tonings. Colour preference is so personal that while some will relish the strong reds and purples, others prefer softer colours.

Single roses are stunning in flower and among the best are Dainty Bess (prominent red stamens against clear pink petals); Wild Flower (recurrent cream blooms on low spreading bush); Macrantha (large clear white blooms with yellow stamens on low spreading shrub); Complicata (large bright pink blooms in abundance on tall spreading shrub); *Rosa laevigata* (robust evergreen climber with large white blooms); and Micrugosa with its large pale pink blooms with yellow stamens.

Striped roses are an acquired taste and lend an old-world aura to the country garden. *Rosa mundi*, Camaieux, Tricolore de Flandre, York and Lancaster, George Vibert, La Rubanee and Honorine de Brabant are among the most beautiful of the striped roses. For more unusual roses, the Green Rose of China (Viridiflora) has double green blooms streaked with red and bronze; and the Wing Thorn Rose (Omeinsis Pteracantha) has unusual translucent red broad-based prickles when young and striking single white blooms. Paulii has white single flowers almost clematis-like in appearance.

Roses suited to covering unsightly buildings or other structures include the bounteous Mme. Alfred Carriere with her wonderfully fragrant double cream blooms throughout the season;

Nancy Hayward (stunning brilliant carmine single blooms throughout the season on evergreen bush); Aimee Vibert (vigorous, almost evergreen climber with white double blooms);

BELOW: Honeyflow is an Australian-bred rose with small, single blooms throughout summer.

OPPOSITE: Rosa mundi (Rosa gallica versicolor) is a wonderful hedging rose with striking blooms. One of the oldest striped roses, it has few thorns and flowers in great abundance.

Felicite et Perpetue (evergreen with creamy white fragrant flowers); Frances E. Lester (floriferous apple blossom blooms followed by masses of brightly coloured heps); Cecile Brunner (pink, fragrant, recurrent dainty blooms on evergreen bush); Constance Spry (spectacular double pink cupped blooms) and the multiflora and sempervirens ramblers.

For the front borders, free flowering shrubs with attractive growth habit are most suited. Many of the David Austin roses are ideal for this purpose: Heritage, The Yeoman, The Friar, Belle Story and Moonbeam. Honeyflow, Carabella and Ballerina are modern shrub roses with delicate single flowers; Penelope, Felicia, Cornelia, Moonlight, Pax and Buff Beauty are popular hybrid musk roses; and Fritz Nobis, Belle Isis, Boule de Neige and La Reine Victoria are perennial favourites.

TREES

ABOVE: Elms carpet the ground with their golden leaves in autumn, providing rich mulch to deter the growth of any unwanted weeds.

OPPOSITE: Trees underplanted with vast drifts of daffodils make an unparalleled sight for the outer boundaries of the country garden.

Trees form the backbone of the country garden, lending character and visual appeal to the landscape. They add height, perspective, shade, shelter and impart an overall framework. There is no doubt that even one or two established trees in a garden will add greatly to its overall ambience. Those starting

LEFT: This mature plane tree lends an aura of stateliness to this large country garden.
OPPOSITE: Trees are not always grown for purely decorative reasons in the country. This Pinus radiata provides shade and shelter for a valued working sheep dog.

a garden from scratch are wise to select a site where they may take advantage of mature trees, saving years of nurturing, and lending an air of establishment.

Apart from their purely aesthetic appeal, in rural areas trees are essential for shade or shelter from winds; for blocking unsightly objects or unwanted views; and for many gardeners they provide valuable produce in the form of fruit and nuts.

There are few gardeners who can visualise the spread of a tree in maturity. Perhaps we are all too preoccupied with immediate results and find it hard to leave such large open spaces needed for many trees to grow into. The great Australian landscape designer, Edna Walling, was a great advocate of deliberate

overplanting in the initial stages, using fast growing species as fill-in or nursery plants. These plants were later to be sacrificed in the name of design, but few of her clients had the heart to do so after years of nuturing. Thus many of her gardens were thought to be over-planted. If a tree has been planted and tended by a garden owner it is not easy to come to terms with its removal. It is far easier to be objective about removing trees that have been planted by others.

There are a myriad varieties of trees to choose from—so where to start? Deciduous for winter sun and summer shade; conifers for structural form; eucalypts for dappled shade and texture; and evergreen for winter pleasure. There are trees with

splendid autumn foliage, or brilliant berries, some with exquisite blossom, a number that attract birds, variegateds for something unusual, and so many differing textures, foliage, bark and shapes. Given this wide choice, there are few gardeners without certain preferences. While some lean towards the exotics, others favour natives; some prefer evergreens to deciduous and others distinctly dislike fastigiates, favouring those with a rounded canopy.

Eminent garden writer, Joan Law-Smith writes: 'I like to think of a garden as one would the composition of a symphony orchestra—not one where each instrument is playing a different noisy tune, a perpetual *fortissimo*, but as a concert of a harmonious whole where a certain tree or plant is wont to play a solo part on occasions, always in tune with the other instruments of its surroundings'. How to achieve such restful harmony? It is not only in colour accord, but in size, shape, texture and even in detail of leaf shape. 'An abundance of small leaves', writes Joan Law-Smith, 'unrelieved by larger ones, can be fidgety; too many sword-shaped leaves can look hostile—and some gardeners find repetitive oval leaves boring.'

In the wider expanses of the country garden, choice is not as limited as the town garden. There is far greater scope, even extending into the landscape beyond, with windbreaks and plantings. As in all facets of gardening there is that constant contention between variety and unity. The gardener within us calls out for as many different types as there is space, while the designer plumps for the overall effect. There is great harmony and unity in a garden with a small palette of plants, with broad brush strokes of one species. The home gardener is often not as disciplined. This is perhaps more apparent in the country, where there is great generosity in sharing plants from the garden and wayward seedlings will be potted to be given away rather than mown over.

Gardeners with plenty of enthusiasm but little knowledge would do best to visit as many gardens of similar climate as possible, always questioning and jotting down names of pleasing shapes and species. There is no blueprint for what is right or wrong. It is purely a matter of personal preference. Invest in a good illustrated tree manual that has climatic limitations. Don't be afraid to try new planting combinations to make your garden distinctive. I have seen so many groups of 'three silver birch' that I find this particular garden feature has little appeal. I am not overly impressed either by a garden full of specimen trees dotted decoratively around the lawn, but it is refreshing to see a little used tree or lesser known species of a common variety.

Gardeners in the tropics need not worry about 'the winter garden' with its stripped back look of bare branches and stunning

RIGHT: Early morning sun filtering through this massive Pinus radiata.

OPPOSITE: Ancient beech trees, with their enormous trunks, have a powerful, brooding presence.

FOLLOWING PAGES: The ambience of this charming cottage garden is carried through to the front entrance, where a white picket fence sets the mood.

outlines. However, for the many gardeners contending with months of bare-limbed trees, there is greater incentive for added variety. The endeavour is to look for suitable evergreens to use as a backdrop, those that have interesting bark or berries or simply those that have a wonderful skeletal structure.

For most of the year, it is that glorious tapestry of leaves that lends so much character to the garden. As Joan Law-Smith writes so evocatively: 'Leaves can weave for us carpets of the utmost beauty, paint for us pictures in shades no jade or emerald could surpass, and throw a coverlet on beds of earth of materials hard or soft, thick or fine, and oft times fragrant; quilted and stitched with living thread, by some wondrous chemistry and workmanship; as only nature can'.

WALLS AND FENCES

There is no element in a garden that creates such a sense of privacy, or is such a tangible use of architecture, as a wall or hedge. They lend an air of permanence and offer a third dimension in planting.

HA-HA WALLS

Ha-ha walls are one of the most effective yet underrated forms of rural landscaping. To integrate the garden into its natural surroundings and to soften the demarcation of garden and beyond is a demanding task. A ha-ha wall provides such a link between garden and countryside that I am amazed it is so little utilised in rural garden design.

A ha-ha wall is virtually an invisible fence—a sunken retaining wall—so that there is no visible barrier when looking out from the garden. On a naturally sloping site, where the garden falls away from the house, a ha-ha wall is built as a retaining wall, but where the garden is on flatter territory, a trench or ditch is made with a wall supporting the vertical garden side. The wall need only be one metre high (less if there are no cattle, goats or deer). Alternatively, a smaller ha-ha may be erected, with a 'hot wire' (electric fence wire) on the lower edge of the wall to deter stock.

It is quite remarkable to look out from a garden without a fence or barrier. The garden becomes part of the broader landscape, 'borrowing' the vista beyond. This integration of garden and surroundings is so much easier to achieve in country gardens where the house and garden are actually part of the countryside as a whole.

The term 'ha-ha' amuses many who have not heard of it, and yet its popularity dates back to the late 1700s when Lancelot 'Capability' Brown simplified many of the great gardens into landscape parks, sweeping away into the countryside beyond. The eighteenth century English landscaper, Charles Bridgeman, is credited with the introduction of the ha-ha in 1712, allowing gardeners to dispense with walls or fences and treat the entire countryside as part of the overall garden design. Originally spelt 'Ah! Ah!', this was allegedly the exclamation of surprise on falling into one!

Any material may be used in the construction of a ha-ha, as it is not seen from inside the garden. Stone and wood are most widely used as they are usually close to hand, but cement, concrete blocks or brick may be suitable. Look around the surrounding countryside and see what element is commonly available—if there is an abundance of rock close by, then this

The charm of the ha-ha wall lies in its ability to give the feeling that the garden is carried on to the countryside beyond. There is no sense of enclosure or indiction of the garden ending. This ha-ha has been constructed from timber and shows the view from within the garden (opposite) and the construction (above).

An uninterrupted view to the countryside beyond: it is hard to ascertain where garden ends and paddock begins in this country garden. The ha-ha wall has been constructed beyond the parterre, and is quite impossible to see from within the garden (opposite). Built from stone, the ha-ha is quite a work of art when seen from beyond the garden (left).

is easily used. Treated wood (or sleeper slabs) is more costly but easily erected and equally effective. In our garden, an 80 metre long ha-ha wall was constructed in two and a half days—the speed of its construction lying in the fact that all the stone and soil was close at hand. Smooth grey river-washed rock had recently been washed up in a flood in the creek at the base of the wall and tonnes of top soil was easily accessible for loading onto a tipping trailer.

Finishing the top edge of the wall requires attention to detail. With a stone wall, flat paving stone may be laid horizontally so that lawn may be mown right to the edge of the wall. With cement or wooden walls, lawn may be grown to the edge, giving the impression of the lawn disappearing into the paddocks or fields beyond.

The actual construction of a ha-ha is similar to that of a retaining wall. A trench needs to be excavated along the natural contour. Stones, brick, concrete slabs or timber are placed against the slope to hold the wall and top soil packed in as the wall is built to the desired height. The force of the wall acts against the weight of the soil and may be successfully built without mortar. Cement is more likely to crack with any natural soil movement, whereas natural materials are more resilient.

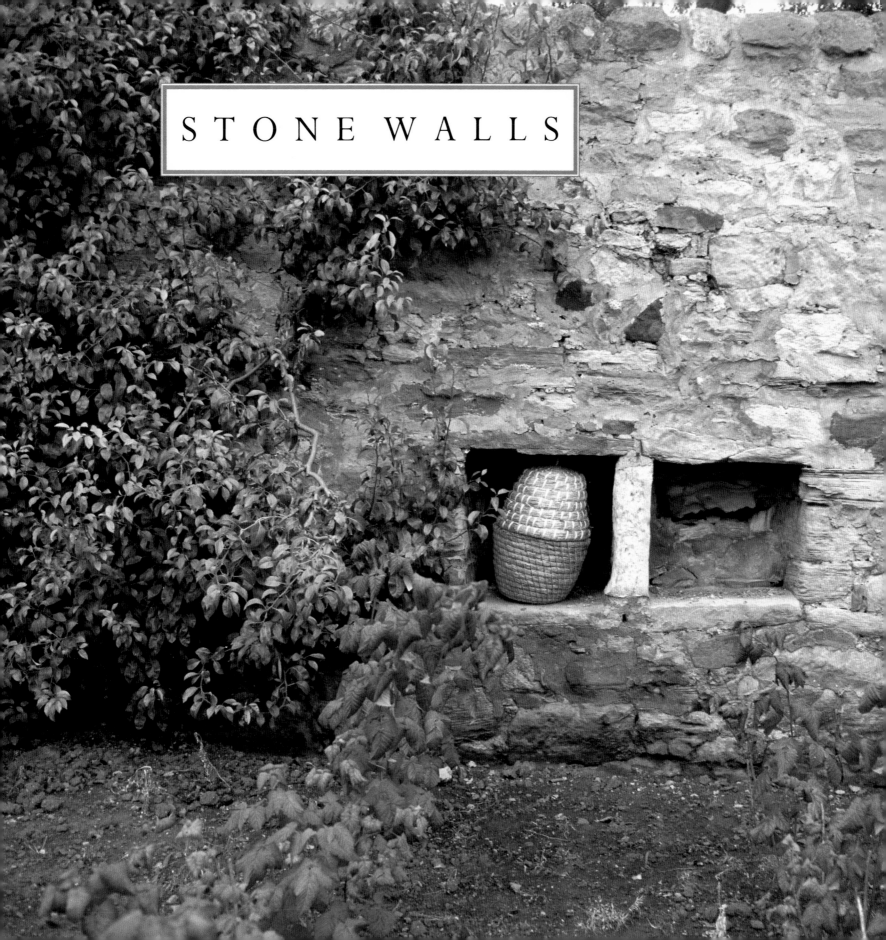

STONE WALLS

N̲o one feature lends such permanence and strength to a garden as a stone wall. Perhaps one of the most durable of all garden structures, they impart a sense of architecture that is enduring. Stone walls are also a wonderful foil for foliage and a mellow backdrop for any planting scheme.

Stone walls are a traditional form of fencing in the country garden, using stone from the surrounding countryside. The sense of structure they impart to a garden is well worth the expense. Although there are no hard and fast rules for selecting an individual type of stone walling, for a natural look, it is important to use local material to blend the garden in with the surroundings. If there is an abundance of slate, use this for all walls, paths and paving within the garden. If there is no local stone, the choice is wider, but keeping the character of the garden in consideration, a formal dressed wall is more appropriate for a classical garden, while a dry stone wall is suitable for an informal country style. Houses constructed from stone may be complemented by walls and paths in the same stone, but contrasting stone could look incongruous.

Walls of differing heights and construction may look inappropriate within a garden. The width and height of the wall is also important. Generally, wide stone walls are more pleasing to the eye than tall narrow ones. A solid wall of one to one

ABOVE: Stone walls look at home in the country garden, imparting a pleasing sense of structure and permanence.
LEFT: Low retaining walls within the garden add interest by creating different levels.
OPPOSITE: The warmth retained in stone walls is here used to advantage to help ripen produce from the kitchen garden.

LEFT: This semi-circular stone wall provides a strong architectural framework within the garden and a pleasing backdrop to trees, lawn and flower borders.
OPPOSITE: This pastoral scene shows how stone houses may be complemented by walls constructed from the same medium.

and a half metres in height is wonderful for sitting on, and makes a splendid addition to any garden. A wall designed for this use needs finishing with a flat coping stone.

Dry stone walling is an age-old art that looks particularly at home in the country garden. Although it takes a craftsman to build a stone wall of distinction as a backdrop in the garden, rather than a focal point, a dry stone wall may be erected by anyone keen enough to try. In many country areas, dry stone walling was the conventional form of fencing, utilising stone gathered from the paddocks. Much of the strength of a dry stone wall lies in its width, which needs to be at least 50 to 60 cm at the base, tapering to 40-50 cm at the top. Rounded river or paddock rocks are usually built in a fairly random fashion, whereas slate or quarried sandstone is usually built into a more formal coursed wall.

Dressed stone walls, quarried and cut by a stonemason, add great distinction to a garden scheme, and are the most durable of all stone walls. Long after planting schemes have changed and matured, the structure of a stone wall provides a sense of antiquity and permanence within the garden. In many old gardens, the walls are the only enduring feature; one that often outlasts many generations of gardeners and plantings.

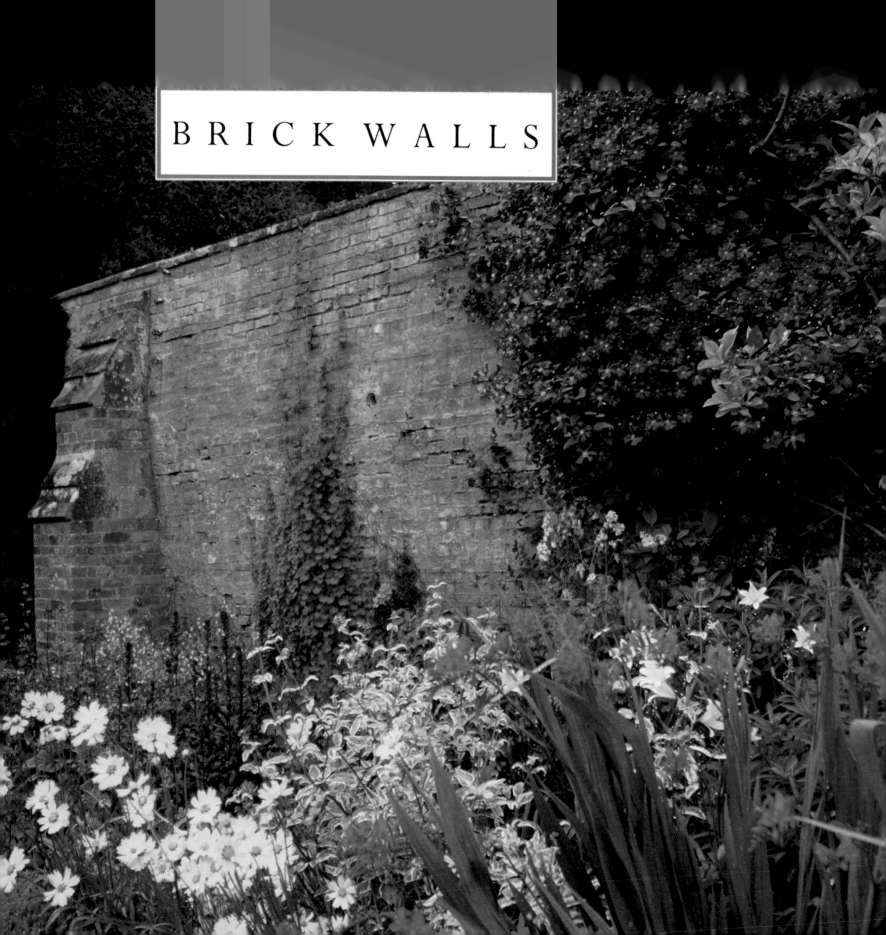

BRICK WALLS

OPPOSITE: *Aged brick walls lend an air of establishment and provide a wonderful backdrop to a herbaceous border.*

ABOVE: *Seven Sisters Rose,* Multiflora platyphylla, *is a tender rambler that requires protection from extreme cold.*

Aged brick walls are among the most alluring of all garden enclosures. A rustic, mellow, tall brick wall, as a backdrop to a mass of greenery, has tremendous appeal. Lending an air of formality, brick walls are not suitable *en masse* for fear of losing their appeal. An entire garden boundary of brick could be overdone in the larger expanse of the country garden, whereas a small walled area could be a highlight of the garden.

Much of the character of a brick wall rests on the style of brick chosen. The texture and colour should complement

ABOVE: Aubretia deltoides grows in the cracks of this aged brick wall. Much of the charm of old brick walls in the garden comes from the lichen and moss growth on them. Reputedly, this growth may be encouraged by painting with sour milk or yoghurt, or, if you can bear the aroma, diluted cow manure!

ABOVE: An ornamental cherry marks the entrance to this brick-walled garden.

the surrounding buildings and garden rather than dominate the setting. Aged brick looks far more interesting and is worth the effort of finding. Where suitable bricks are unobtainable, a lime wash, whitewash or bagged effect mellows and ages a new wall in an established garden scheme.

Brick walls are relatively easy to build, but need to be well-constructed with adequate foundations. They need to not only look substantial but be solid in construction—at least two bricks in width. A single brick wall looks flimsy and inadequate. Height

is also vital and a tall wall has far greater appeal than a stubby, suburban-looking wall. Joints should not be too deeply raked and the mortar should not look too much like cement in colour.

A brick wall gives a great feeling of permanence to a garden. The sense of enclosure emanating from such a structure adds much to the ambience of the garden. Using one wall of a house or outbuilding, only two more are needed to create a courtyard enclosure, providing protection from prevailing winds, a suntrap in winter and a place to grow more treasured plants. Brick retains its warmth and plants growing against such a wall will thrive.

A brick enclosure may be suited for a winter garden, filled with winter-flowering plants such as helleborus, daphnes, winter sweet, winter-flowering viburnums, violets, magnolias, camellia sasanqua, winter honeysuckle with espaliered winter-flowering prunus (*Prunus subhirtella* or *serrulata*) or japonica against the walls and *Iris unguicularis* at their base. The fragrance and beauty of these plants throughout the winter months, added to the shelter and privacy of a solid enclosure, makes a delightful feature for any garden.

LEFT: This curved brick wall and lampstand provide a private side entrance to this country home.
OPPOSITE: Picket fencing has great appeal as a front entrance, but the upkeep often precludes it from being used to enclose the entire boundary of large gardens.

PICKET FENCES

Pickets are a traditional form of fencing in the country and many are seen in old country gardens or around smaller farmhouses. They lend a nostalgic air to the garden, adding to its charm. However they are not by any means maintenance free, and this precludes their presence from many gardens. To keep their neat, crisp appearance they require frequent repainting and in large country gardens, this is often not feasible or desirable. An unpainted paling fence has a different kind of appeal, with

ABOVE: Painted wooden pickets with decorative tops rise out of a sea of Erigeron. OPPOSITE: Hollyhocks and picket fences seem to represent the quintessence of the cottage garden.

its weathered grey wood blending in to the garden background and requires no maintenance—but will not have as long a life as a painted fence.

Much of the charm of the picket fence is in the glimpse of the garden through the pickets; alternatively, looking from the garden to the countryside beyond. So great is their appeal and variation in design, a span of picket fencing may be used at the front entrance; on either side of the entrance gate or ramp; or perhaps along one side of the garden, separating the garden from outbuildings. Substantial enough to prevent stock entering the garden, a picket fence provides an effective wind barrier, while adding to the attractiveness of the garden.

Easily constructed, the pickets are simply nailed on to a simple timber framework. Much of the pleasure of constructing such a fence is deciding on the style of picket. Most simple styles may be purchased pre-cut while others may be shaped

by the home builder. The simple pointed Gothic style is the traditional picket of the cottage garden and may be far more effective than a more fanciful design. Diagonally sawn or rounded top pickets have a simple charm, while some of the carved designs lend a greater air of distinction. Picket fences with undulating tops look wonderful when combined with dressed posts with turned finials or capped tops. A wooden picket gate completes the scheme.

The variety of pickets and styles of picket fences is so extensive that, if you are contemplating such a fence, take

Picket fences with undulating decorative tops may dress up a front entrance (above); however the simple pointed picket has great charm in old gardens (opposite), seen here as a backdrop to a formal herb garden.

FOLLOWING PAGES: Harvesting herbs and flowers is part of the joy of country gardening. Here, seed heads from poppies, love-in-a-mist and garlic are drying with blue delphiniums, lemon verbena, white borage, thyme, mint, achillea and lavender.

photographs, do sketches and experiment with varied styles on paper before deciding. Colour is also an important consideration. While the traditional picket fence is painted white, this is not always sympathetic to the rural surroundings, and a soft grey-green, dark green or umber painted fence may blend in with greater effect.

PRODUCE

The bounteous nature of the country garden is one of its delights. There is often an overabundance, whether it is flowers, vegetables or fruit, and there is a genuine pleasure in sharing the spoils.

ORCHARDS

There is something immensely pleasing about strolling in a country orchard—the trees laden with fruit or bees swarming around the fragrant blossom. The long lines of trees in orderly precision is delightful in its simplicity. A feeling of intimacy adds another dimension to an orchard if the area is bordered by a tall hawthorn or fruiting hedge planted as a windbreak.

The scale of country gardens is such that a separate orchard may be incorporated into the garden boundary. Although fruit and nut trees need not necessarily be confined solely to the orchard, there is something immensely pleasing in the orderliness and productivity of such an area. The orchard need not be totally utilitarian, but may be enhanced with long grass walks; sweeps of bulbs; and vistas to the countryside beyond.

The orchard need not be hidden from view, but can become a feature of the country garden. An avenue of pear or quince trees leading to the house or outbuildings has great panache, and a cherry or plum walk has old world charm. An orchard may be made into a wild garden with meandering pathways leading through a mass of wildflowers or forget-me-nots. An orchard in spring with trees laden in blossom and petals carpeting the ground is an ethereal sight; and mid-summer, laden with fruit, an enticing place to take a walk. Many of the deciduous fruit trees have wonderful autumn foliage and even in winter, the bare branches and stripped back look has a pleasing quality. The beauty of apple, quince and pear blossom; autumn foliage of persimmon, medlar, quince, pear and apricot; spreading shade of walnut, almond, pear and apricot is enhanced when planted *en masse*.

RIGHT: Pears ripen with help from the heat generated by these old stone walls.
OPPOSITE: Bulbs naturalise in this apple orchard with great charm.

The taste of fruit picked straight from the tree is unparalleled, and any excess may be bottled or made into jams, chutneys, sauces or jellies. There is also pleasure in having friends and neighbours pick the surplus. This bounteous nature of the country garden is one of its delights. There is often an overabundance, whether it is flowers, vegetables or fruit, and there is a genuine pleasure in sharing the spoils.

While orchards are traditionally the place for growing fruit, there is certainly no need to confine such productive trees solely to a separate area. Planted within the garden, their blossom, shade and foliage is comparable to many deciduous trees, with the great bonus of a harvest of fresh fruit. Fruit trees within the garden are more attractive if not pruned severely, so they take on the shape of a shade tree rather than a purely utilitarian bearer of produce.

Country gardens with limited space may find a challenge in espaliering trees in rows or along fences, walls or buildings. Fruiting grape vines may be grown over pergolas or arches, and currants and berries trained into hedges. Growing fruit trees in large pots has been practised throughout the ages by the ancient Persians, Greeks and Egyptians and remains an alternative way of growing frost-tender fruit in colder climates. Kumquats, lemons and limes make attractive potted specimens in sheltered courtyards or verandahs, and in warmer climates the pomegranate and pineapple lend themselves to container growing.

LEFT: The bounty of the country garden, where a plentiful harvest means enough produce to eat fresh, or bottle, to make into jams and jellies and to distribute amongst friends. There are great rewards for the gardener who plants fruit or nut trees, in this case, a young nectarine tree provides fruit in abundance.
OPPOSITE: The apple tree, Malus sylvestris, thrives in the cool climate garden. There are many varieties to choose from and rather than relegate them purely to the orchard, they are an attractive ornamental tree, with their wonderful large spring blossom and attractive autumn colouring. In the informal country garden, fruit-bearing trees look striking as the fruit grows to maturity.

For those with more exotic tastes, some of the less common fruits are worth considering, such as loquats, feijoas, lychees, guavas, medlars, olives, persimmons, pomegranates, mulberries and figs. When selecting varieties, seek those suitable to your own climatic region. Bananas, avocadoes, mangoes, guavas, lychees, paw-paws and custard apples are suited to tropical

ABOVE: Early spring in the orchard with yellow and white daffodils carpeting the ground in a tapestry of colour.

OPPOSITE: In the town or country, one of the most rewarding of horticultural pursuits is to make the kitchen garden attractive rather than purely utilitarian. Here, fruit trees provide a soft background to the formal vegetable garden, edged with buxus.

climates, while apples, pears and stone fruit need cooler conditions. Mulching is effective in reducing temperature fluctuations and protecting against excessive loss of moisture from the soil. It has the added advantage of providing nutrients to the soil as it decomposes.

While not all fruit trees need regular pruning, it is advised for optimum quality and quantity. Pest control is another factor, and this does not necessarily mean using poisonous chemicals. Companion planting is an age-old practice of deterring specific pests and weeds and is being backed up by scientific research.

HERBS

The fragrance, flavour, flowers and foliage of herbs make them unparalleled in the plant kingdom. There would be few country gardens without a scattering of herbs amongst the palette of plants. Whether a separate area is set aside for a herb garden or they are used as borders along paths or garden beds; grown within the kitchen garden or in the flower borders; the spectrum of herbs from which to choose is endless.

Such is their charm and hardiness that many herbs form the backbone of the flower bed: the handsome shaggy heads of the bergamot, the downy grey leaves of Lamb's ears, the yellow button heads of santolina, the silver leafed artemesias, the fragrant lavenders, ground covering thymes, the soft white spires of lemon verbena or the sky blue rosemary flowers.

Herbs are among the hardiest of all garden plants and most thrive in the poorest, most gravelly soil in the garden. Suited to most climatic conditions, they thrive in dry times and need little pampering. During prolonged droughts in our garden, I am very grateful for the lavenders, thymes, rosemary, tansy, lemon balm and parsley which never seem to show any signs of heat or water stress.

Lavender is deservedly the most popular herb in the country garden. The fragrant spikes are valued as a picked or dried flower; it is the essential ingredient in most potpourris; its rounded form is attractive year round, and it is wonderful in the flower bed or as a low hedge or border. There can never be enough lavender in the country garden—planted alongside steps, as borders to paths, around the clothes line, in the garden border or edging the kitchen garden. Plant it where its sweet fragrance will be emitted as you brush past. There are many varieties— some white, some pink, others green, many blue or purple, growing on dwarf or tall bushes with spiky or soft flower heads.

Rosemary is one of the most underrated herbs. It should be appreciated, not only for its culinary appeal, but as a handsome shrub with its grey foliage and soft blue flowers. *Rosmarinus officinalis* makes an attractive shapely hedge while the low growing prostrate variety, *Rosmarinus officinalis prostratus* is wonderful for retaining walls or rockeries, or in pots.

Every country garden should have a bay tree (*Laurus nobilis*),

The pleasures of herbs are infinite, and apart from their decorative aspect in the garden (opposite), their colour, fragrance and culinary use make them invaluable in concocting vinegars, oils and potpourris (above).

whether planted within the garden or in a tub that can be sheltered from cold winds or frosts in colder climates. The deep green leaves are favoured by cooks and wreath-makers, and the handsome growing habit makes it an attractive addition to the garden. It is a popular choice for clipping as a centrepiece for a herb garden or for potted standards in a protected courtyard.

The feathery white flowers of garlic chives look wonderful in the flower border amongst roses and perennials, while the

smaller growing common chive, *Allium schoenoprasum* is a popular border in the kitchen garden. The most distinctive and well-known member of the *Allium* family is garlic, with its lofty heads of purple flowers and grey-green strappy foliage. When the foliage has died down at the end of summer, the garlic may be hung in plaits in a cool dry place and used as needed. The seed heads are wonderful in flower arrangements and dry beautifully.

The richly coloured foliage of many of the herbs adds much to a garden scheme with the bronze of bronze fennel; the purple tonings of black peppermint, purple sage and purple basil; the gold foliage of golden marjoram and dill; variegated leaves of some varieties of thyme and elderberry and the silver-grey tonings of many lavenders, santolina, sage, artemesia and rosemary. The feathery heads of sweet cicely, dill, fennel and angelica add texture

to the garden while the stately spires of *Verbascum* or bergamot add height and interest.

Designing a herb garden is one of the most exciting tasks in the garden. Whatever the style of the rest of the garden, the herb garden may take its own identity. The herb garden is one area where a little whimsy in the form of geometrically shaped beds or parterre may be used without upsetting the balance of the entire garden. An enticing potager with neat borders of herbs may be the *pièce de résistance* of an otherwise informal country garden. The exuberant growth and gentle interplay of foliage colour imparts a picturesque effect year-round. The formality of an intricately designed potager is softened by the abundant greenery and profuse flowering.

The most important consideration when planning a herb garden or just popping a couple of favourite herbs in the flower beds, is that they should be placed strategically close to the kitchen. Even a few pots on the windowsill or at the back door is enough for day-to-day use. There is greater incentive to sprinkle herbs through your cooking if they are close at hand. Planning a herb garden within constant view of the kitchen is one of the best ideas for easy accessability and as an incentive for keeping it in order. The most looked-upon garden beds are usually those kept in best order. Growing in wild abandon or in formal knot patterns, herbs are a great asset to the garden, both for their foliage and flowers as well as their culinary use.

THE KITCHEN GARDEN

Country dwellers tend to be among the most practical of gardeners. Perhaps it is purely the convenience factor—the necessity of having produce at hand when needed. The country dweller so often has to 'make do'—whipping up meals for unexpected guests when the pantry is bare. There is also the freshness of home grown produce—for many country people, trips to the shops are irregular and produce may already be days old when purchased—offering no comparison to the taste and freshness of vegetables picked straight from the garden.

A kitchen garden is a natural extension of the country garden, even if it is only a few rows of carrots or permanent plantings of rhubarb and asparagus. There is something immensely pleasing about the orderliness of the kitchen garden—rows of greenery and that wonderful sense of productivity. Although we often hear of the cottager's penchant for growing the vegetables in with the flowers, it is in fact far easier and makes more sense to grow them in a more orderly fashion in an area set aside solely for their production.

This does not mean the kitchen garden need be drab—far from it. Edged with borders of lavender, rosemary or chives, with perhaps a friendly scarecrow for fun and a birdbath for the birds to play in, or filled with plants selected for their foliage and form, such as the globe artichoke, there is much to recommend it for pure aesthetics alone. For many, the kitchen garden becomes an art form, with espaliered fruit trees, hedges of berries, intricate layouts and clipped borders. One only has to look at photographs of Château de Villandry in France—

BELOW: The kitchen garden becomes an art form to the truly ambitious and this immaculately kept and planned garden is a paragon of productivity, design and orderliness.

OPPOSITE: A 'no-dig' vegetable patch has been grown on the cement verandah of this old farm building.

a formal potager where vegetables are chosen for their colour and arranged in a reconstruction of a sixteenth-century garden. On a more achievable scale, the Heide Kitchen Garden in Melbourne is wonderful, with its network of gravel paths and feeling of enclosure from the rose-covered fence surrounding the garden.

The structural framework and tidiness of the kitchen garden are much of the appeal, but require constant vigilance to achieve a good result. There is no denying the time and energy needed—

ABOVE: Globe artichokes, Cynara scolymus, *are the most decorative of plants in the kitchen garden, with their rosettes of enormous silver-grey leaves and large thistle like flowers. Stunning in flower, this perennial is also used as a background in the flower border.*

OPPOSITE: The ultimate in kitchen garden design is the walled garden, though it is more suited to cool climates, where the walls provide shelter and radiate warmth.

ABOVE: This fleshy, leaf-like head is the edible portion of the globe artichoke, Cynara scolymus, *much favoured by gourmets.*

OPPOSITE: A low stone wall provides a pleasing backdrop to this productive vegetable border.

vegetable gardens are rarely minimum care. This is, hopefully, outweighed by the sense of accomplishment and joy derived from eating your own produce.

Growing produce not commonly available is another incentive to venture into the kitchen garden. Witloof, winged beans, endive, purslane and ornamental kale are among the many more exotic varieties to try. An intriguing concept is growing mesclun salad greens. An art practiced by the French for hundreds of years, a selection of mixed salad greens are grown in the same row. These are picked while small and tender (4-6 weeks after sowing), make a tasty and innovative salad, and also look wonderful in the garden. Mesclun seed mix may be purchased ready-made or made to order from a selection of red and green

loose-leaf lettuce, endive, chervil, aragula, cress, mustard, purslane, sorrel, fennel, orach and leaf celery.

Sunlight is the one essential ingredient in the vegetable garden. Soils may be improved, layouts played around with, fertilisers added, crops rotated or mulching carried out, but the one requisite is adequate sunlight—five hours minimum. Any more than this will enhance maturity and sweetness and any less will retard growth and result in sour-tasting produce. Rows ideally should be planted running north-south to receive most sunlight.

Paths are essential in the vegetable garden. As constant watering is needed, it is frustrating to have to tramp through sodden ground to pick the vegetables for the evening meal. Gravel or straw keep service areas mud free. Paths may be lined with bricks, stone or timber, or edged with thyme, strawberries or chives. Paths are useful in dividing the different areas and for easy access when weeding and picking.

As one of the greatest benefits of home-grown vegetables is that they are healthier and tastier to eat, it seems farcical to smother them in chemicals. Companion planting is a far easier and healthier alternative (see page 152). Strong, robust plants have far better resistance to attack than poor undernourished specimens, so compost and fertiliser are important additions. Crop rotation may also help break the disease cycle. In simple terms, this means not planting the same vegetable in the same position each year.

Positioning the kitchen garden is all important. Don't be reluctant to move the site if it has become too shady. Although the soil of an existing site may have been built up for years with compost and mulch, it is surprising how vegetables thrive in a new site.

The traditional method of fork, spade and aching back is not the ideal way to start a new area. There is a far easier, more effective method, utilising five items usually on hand in a country garden—straw, lucerne hay, compost, chook manure and newspapers. A 'no-dig' garden may be prepared in no time at all using these ingredients, producing vegetables in an almost weed-free environment. Esther Deans, who pioneered this method

in Australia has had startling results and has a huge following. Basically, such a garden entails laying a thick wad of newspaper, topped with pads of lucerne hay and a dusting of organic fertiliser. This is covered with about 20 cm of loose straw and another sprinkling of fertiliser. A circle of rich compost is then put where each seed is to be planted. Putting a leafy crop, such as zucchini, squash or pumpkin is a good way to start the process, followed by a root crop, such as carrots or parsnips. It is also the ideal way to grow potatoes, starting them in a little compost under the straw. Having used this method, there is never any need to go back to the traditional back-breaking task of continually digging the vegetable garden.

The kitchen garden is perhaps the most time-consuming area in the garden, so it is wise to keep gardening methods here as simple as possible. By doing away with all the chemicals that need such timely vigilance in application and the charts and diagrams detailing complicated crop rotation calendars, and concentrating entirely on planting for maximum nutrition, there are great rewards to be reaped. The one important factor, which changes from district to district, is a sowing calendar. Local advice may mean the difference between enjoying the vegetable garden or being totally disheartened by the poor results from sowing crops unsuited to the climatic conditions.

N A T U R A L
F A R M I N G

Natural farming is really a return to traditional farming methods, before the advent of harmful chemicals and poisons. The quest for 'bigger' and 'better' has flooded the market with chemical sprays and dusts that have not been welcomed by all gardeners. For the environmentally aware and those wishing the food they eat to be free from artificial chemicals, there has been a return to basics.

Many of the farming methods practiced by our forebears are once again being used, under the term permaculture or organic farming. A natural balance is once again being sought. The use of harmful chemicals disrupts this essential balance of minerals, nutrients, insects and bacteria within the soil. High yields are not so much the aim as producing vitamin-rich, clean, healthy produce, free from artificial residues.

Natural farming does not mean doing away with fertilisers, pest controls and mulch. It simply means choosing those that are gentle on the soil, without harming the micro-organisms and worms that are essential for healthy soil. Use of artificial fertilisers promotes unnaturally lush growth, which is far more susceptible to disease and pests. Continued use of artificial inorganic fertilisers may harm soil organisms and change the pH level, whereas organic fertilisers, such as animal manure, compost and blood and bone enhance the soil structure.

Organic matter is the basis of good soil structure. More than any other area in the garden, the vegetable patch needs to be constantly reworked. This continued digging may damage the soil profile and adversely affect drainage, but this may be remedied by maintaining a good level of organic matter— particularly animal manure, which has a slow-release action. This organic matter eventually becomes humus which effectively acts as a sponge, absorbing surplus water and slowly releasing it to the plants as needed.

One of the most overlooked means of building soil fertility is growing a green manure crop such as lupins, clover, dun peas or tick beans. These are dug into the soil when flowering, adding nitrogen and organic matter for future crops. This is best done during the relatively fallow winter period when the vegetable garden is not full to overflowing. A mixture of legumes and

OPPOSITE: This copper, long past its usefulness in the laundry, is evocative of the simpler, traditional life on the farm.

ABOVE: Geese make a useful addition to the country garden, keeping snails and pests away.

cereal crops may be planted in autumn and dug into the soil in spring to help regenerate nutrients.

While green manure crops and organic fertilisers improve the soil structure, mulch is used to reduce water loss and keep roots cool. Natural mulches such as hay, straw, grass clippings, compost, leaves and sawdust enrich the soil as they break down, whereas mulches, such as black plastic, stones, brick or weed mats do not enhance soil structure.

An understanding of crop rotation negates the necessity for harmful chemicals and helps reduce the depletion of certain soil elements. Continuous plantings of root crops may lead to a phosphorous deficiency, while successive plantings of leaf crops can use up the nitrogen supply in the soil. Soil-borne diseases may result in low-yielding stunted yellow plants. Where a disease has taken hold and even crop rotation seems to have little effect, an intervention crop such as oats may break the life cycle, if dug into the soil while still green. Gladioli is also said to reduce the severity of white root rot in onions. Many gardeners use the kitchen garden to grow bulbs such as gladioli or flowers for picking that may not have a place in the garden proper. This not only brightens up the vegetable patch, but may form part of the rotation cycle or be used as companion plants.

Harsh chemicals may be replaced by natural sprays, using garlic, wood ashes or pyrethrum, or more simply by attracting predators that live off common insect pests. Such predators will never rid the garden entirely of pests, but will help keep them at tolerable levels. Most predatory insects need plants rich in pollen and nectar.

LEFT: In addition to their role in pest control, chickens and geese are a valuable source of manure for the garden, and eggs and meat for the gardener.

OPPOSITE: Collecting leaf mulch is one of the joys of autumn. Leaf mulch is one of the most valuable natural assets available to the gardener, either to add to the compost or to put around trees and shrubs to deter weed growth and to conserve moisture.

One of the oldest tried and true natural farming practices is allowing chooks into the orchard where they scavenge fallen fruit and larvae or pupae of pests. They are efficient at converting plants to protein by helping control weedy vegetation and providing one of the most sought after manures. Pigs may also be used to forage windfall fruits once trees are semi-established (at least three years old). Sheep may be used to graze the orchard area, providing they do not damage the trees.

Basically all permaculture and organic farming practices are based on natural systems in harmony with nature. Rather than doing battle with our surrounds there is pride in using our natural resources to their full potential.

COMPANION PLANTING

ABOVE AND OPPOSITE: Companion planting at its best—flowers, vegetables and herbs together in a wonderfully productive garden. In their natural state, flowers and vegetables grow happily together. Many flowers are beneficial to neighbouring vegetables, keeping them free from pestilent insects and in some cases, improving their flavour. Many gardeners still favour the kitchen garden as the place to grow their brightly coloured flowers for the house, a 'picking garden' and this brightens up the vegetable patch immeasurably.

With a general awareness growing of the harm of chemicals and poisons to the environment and in the soil, the age-old art of companion planting is being looked at more seriously. By simply growing compatible plants alongside each other, pests and weeds are deterred and plants are seen to flourish.

Companion planting evolved from the cottage gardeners of long ago, when vegetables were planted with flowers. This was

ABOVE: Marigolds, Tagetes, *are one of the most popular companion plants, deterring predators and clearing the ground of many destructive nematodes. Here they have been used extensively in this large geometrically designed kitchen garden.*

OPPOSITE: For pure aesthetics alone, there is much in favour of colourful flowers in the kitchen garden.

not purely for aesthetic reasons; it is known that monocultures allow pests and diseases to spread rapidly, whereas mixed cultures are more resistant and provide a more bounteous harvest, both in terms of flowers and vegetables. Gardens devoted entirely to roses for example, will be prone to aphid infestation; by planting garlic or chives nearby, aphids are deterred. This

traditional gardening know-how was handed down from generation to generation of gardeners and has been the basis for much of our current knowledge.

Soil nutrition is an important aspect of a healthy garden, and composting, mulching and crop rotation are all aids to companion planting. High fertility and rotation of crops help control pests and diseases. By moving plants from plot to plot, any soil-borne pests or diseases are unable to survive without their host plants. Certain plants are good companions as they disguise the scent of their neighbouring plants or act as decoys, while others reduce nematodes within the soil or act as hosts to predators that live off insect pests, while others may be used for safe home-made insecticides.

One of the wonders of nature is the balance between pests and predators. Where one insect is a problem, others can be attracted to counteract and prey on the pest. Aphids, for example, are a common pest, but can be controlled by ladybirds, lacewings and hoverflies. These need plants rich in nectar and pollen to supplement their aphid diet, and if such plants are within the garden then the predators will keep the aphids in check. Fortunately, most of the flowers predators are attracted to are popular garden plants, such as sunflowers, goldenrod, mint, hyssop or fennel. These will not only provide splashes of colour but will attract many aphid-eating insects.

While there are some plants that attract predators to prey on the insect pests, there are those plants that actually repel, kill or deter pests. Horseradish and dandelions are said to deter chewing beetles; carrots deter onion flies; wormwood deters mice, slugs and snails; rosemary makes a wonderful kitchen garden border deterring bean beetles, cabbage moths, carrot flies and many other insects; and tansy deters many insects including ants, aphids, cabbage worms, chewing beetles, Japanese beetles and squash bugs.

Many herbs are beneficial to plant health and may be grown to aid the growth of other plants: hyssop, lovage, marjoram, tarragon, thyme and yarrow. Some herbs are said to improve the flavour of nearby vegetables, such as summer savoury planted near beans and cucumbers and winter savoury near onions.

Some herbs are handy to keep at the back door to keep away insects and pests—even snakes! The strong fragrance of rue and tansy acts as a fly repellent; tansy and pennyroyal keep ants at bay; and lad's love is said to deter snakes! Basil is said to protect tomatoes while horseradish guards potatoes. The purple flowers of hyssop keep cabbage moths away while parsley is a wonderful neighbour to roses, tomatoes and asparagus.

Not all companion plants are those normally grown in the garden. Some wild flowers, grasses or legumes are good nitrogen fixers. Lupins, clovers and lucerne are among those that take nitrogen from the air and 'fix' it in the soil. Their deep roots are also good for breaking up the soil and making it more friable.

While there are good companions, there are also those that are not so happy in each other's company. Potatoes grown at

the base of apple trees are said to have a negative effect; strawberries do not like having cabbage, cauliflower, broccoli or brussel sprouts nearby; asparagus shouldn't be grown near onions; parsley and mint are not good companions; grapes do not like cabbage or radish nearby; and raspberries are averse to blackberry or potato neighbours.

The greater the diversity of plants, the greater the number of insects present. Research shows that predators are likely to outweigh pests in a normal garden situation. With a wide range of plants there will be greater diversity of insect life, and far less chance of any one pest overrunning the garden.

LEFT: A farm truck, loaded with bales of wool, provides a rural backdrop to this rose garden.

ABOVE: Garlic is a favoured plant in the garden, not only for its attractive seed head, but for its ability to discourage disease and bugs, such as Rose aphids and Japanese beetles.

ACKNOWLEDGEMENTS

My thanks to the many people who have made it possible for this book to be published; the many gardeners and designers on both sides of the globe who have created such images of beauty that have inspired the photographs in this book; the publishers who mould the book from disparate photographs into such a volume; and my family who put up with my photographic wanderings and time spent in the precinct of my office.

My thanks to Betty Osborne, Joan Massy, Jim and Ann Maslin, James and Barbara Litchfield, Betty Casey-Litchfield, Stephanie and Patrick Litchfield, Jim and Libby Litchfield, John and Bev Allen, Mick and Oenone Larritt, Geoff and Joy Cottle, David and Gay Epstein, Pat and Judy Bowley, Rob Tooth, Hugh Bligh, Margaret Darling, Ann Snow, Helen Watson, Jenny Mckay, Joan Downes, the Ryrie family, Jo Gordon, Brian and Marcia Voce, Peter and Kate Gullett, Butch and Willy Shannon, Jim and Eve Harris, Diana Lempriere, Helen Gordon, Luki Weatherly, Sue Manifold, Elizabeth Gilfillan, Mrs I.D. MacKinnon, Mrs Murray, Mr and Mrs Frank Walker, Maurie and Trish Bull, Elaine Lawson (Lanyon Historic Homestead, Museums Unit, A.C.T. Government), Penny Hoskins, Rowena Weir, Jackie Armes, Jan Wagstaff, Annie Snodgrass, Robin Jeffcoat, Liz Kelly, Margie Knight-Gregson, Fiona Masey, Heather Haylock, Marg Herbert; photographers Lorna Rose, Paul Clarke, Paul Foley and Joy Harland, Vision Graphics processing and the Schoo family in Cooma; on the publishing side, my thanks to Kim Anderson, Garth Nix, Nicole Court and Liz Seymour; and to my family, Darvall, Skye and Hamish, promise of more time in the kitchen and less in the garden and office!

BIBLIOGRAPHY

BIRD, Richard, *Companion Planting*. Simon and Schuster, Australia, 1991

BISGROVE, Richard, *The Flower Garden*. Collins Publishers, Sydney, 1989

BLIGH, Beatrice, *Cherish the Earth*. Ure Smith, Sydney 1973

——, *Down to Earth*. Angus and Robertson, Sydney, 1968

BROOKES, John, *The Country Garden*. Dorling Kindersley, London, 1987

——, *Your Garden Design Book*. Lothian Publishing, Australia, 1991

BROWN, Jane, *Vita's Other World: A Gardening Biography of Vita Sackville-West*. Penguin, 1987

——, *Gardens of a Golden Afternoon*. Penguin, 1987

CAPEK, Karel, *The Gardener's Year*. Allen and Unwin, London, 1931

CUFFLEY, Peter, *Cottage Gardens in Australia*. Five Mile Press, Melbourne, 1983

——, *Creating Your Own Period Garden*. Five Mile Press, 1984

DEANS, Esther, *Esther Deans' Gardening Book: growing without digging*. Harper and Row, 1977

DIXON, Trisha, *The Essence of the Garden: Garden Design and Style*. CollinsAngus and Robertson, Australia, 1991

DIXON, Trisha & **CHURCHILL**, Jennie, *Gardens in Time: In the Footsteps of Edna Walling*. Angus and Robertson, Sydney, 1988

FELTWELL, John, *The Naturalist's Garden*. Ebury Press, 1987

GARNETT, Tom, *Man of Roses*. Kangaroo Press, Australia, 1990

GALBRAITH, Jean, *Garden in a Valley*. Five Mile Press, Victoria, 1985

——, *A Garden Lover's Journal 1943–1946*. Five Mile Press, 1989

GRIFFITHS, Trevor, *My World of Old Roses*. Whitcoulls Publishers, Christchurch (NZ), 1983

HARRIS, Thistle, *Wild Flowers of Australia*. Angus and Robertson Publishers, 1986

HOBHOUSE, Penelope, *Garden Style*. Frances Lincoln Ltd, 1988

——, *The Country Gardener*. Frances Lincoln Ltd, 1989

——, (ed), *Gertrude Jekyll on Gardening*. Vintage Books, 1985

HUTCHISON, Frances, *Landscaping with Perennials*. Angus and Robertson, Australia, 1988

INNES, Miranda, *The Passionate Gardener*. Ebury Press, London, 1990

JEKYLL, Gertrude, *The Making of a Garden*. Antique Collectors' Club, 1984

—— (with Edward Mawley), *Roses for English Gardens*. Penguin Books, 1983

JOHNSON, Hugh, *The Principles of Gardening*. Mitchell Beazley, London, 1979

JOYCE, David, *Garden Styles: An Illustrated History of Design and Tradition*. Pyramid Books, 1989

KELLY, Frances, *A Simple Pleasure: the art of garden making in Australia*. Methuen Australia, 1982

KNIGHT, Margaret, *Mice Don't Like Spearmint*. William Heinemann Australia, 1990

LACEY, Stephen, *The Startling Jungle*. Penguin, 1987

LATREILLE, Anne, *The Natural Garden. Ellis Stones: His Life and Work*. Viking O'Neill, Ringwood, 1990

LAW-SMITH, Joan, *The Uncommon Garden*. The Women's Committee of the National Trust of Australia (Vic), 1983

—— , *A Gardener's Diary*, The Women's Committee of the National Trust (Vic) 1976

—— , *The Garden Within*, The Women's Committee of the National Trust (Vic) 1991

LLOYD, Christopher & **BIRD**, Richard, *The Cottage Garden*. Dorling Kindersley, London, 1990

MACOBOY, Stirling, *What Tree is That?*. Tiger Books International Ltd, London, 1986

MANSFIELD, T.C. *The Border in Colour*. Collins, London, 1947

MASSINGHAM, Betty, *Miss Jekyll*. David and Charles, London, 1966

McLEOD, Judyth, *Our Heritage of Old Roses*. Kangaroo Press, Sydney, 1987

MOLLISON, Bill & **HOLMGREN**, David, *Permaculture One: A Perennial Agriculture for Human Settlements*. Tagari Publications, Australia, 1982

MOLLISON, Bill with **RENY**, Mia Slay, *Introduction to Permaculture*. Tagari Publications, Australia, 1991

MURRAY, Elizabeth & **FELL**, Derek, *Home Landscaping . . . Ideas, Styles and Designs for Creative Outdoor Spaces*. Simon and Schuster, New York

NICHOLS, Beverley, *Down the Garden Path*. Pan Books, London, 1950

NICHOLSON, Nigel, *Portrait of a Marriage*. Weidenfeld and Nicolson, London, 1983

NICHOLSON, Phillipa (ed), *Vita Sackville-West's Garden Book*. Atheneum, New York, 1968

NOTTLE, Trevor, *Growing Old-Fashioned Roses in Australia and New Zealand*. Kangaroo Press, 1983

OSLER, Mirabel, *A Gentle Plea for Chaos*. Bloomsbury, London, 1989

PAGE, Russell, *The Education of a Gardener*. Penguin Books, London, 1985

PAUL, Anthony & **REES**, Yvibbe, *The Garden Design Book*. Collins, London, 1988

PHILLIPS, Roger, *Trees in Britain, Europe and North America*. Pan Books, 1978

PHILLIPS, Roger & **RIX**, Martyn, *Roses*. Pan Books, London, 1988

PIRIE, Chris, *The Australian Scented Garden*. Harper and Row, Sydney, 1984

PROUDFOOT, Helen, *Gardens in Bloom*. Kangaroo Press 1989

READER'S DIGEST, *Gardeners' Encyclopaedia of Plants and Flowers*. Reader's Digest (Australia), 1991

ROBINSON, Joyce, *Glorious Disarray: The Creation of a Garden*. Michael Joseph, London, 1990

ROBINSON, William, *The Wild Garden*. Century Hutchison/The National Trust, London, 1983

——, *English Flower Garden*. Amaryllis Press, 1984

ROSE, Graham, *The Romantic Garden*. William Collins, Australia 1988
——, *The Traditional Garden Book*. Greenhouse Publications, Australia, 1989
SACKVILLE-WEST, Vita, *The Garden*. Michael Joseph, London, 1946
SAVILLE, Diana, *Gardens for Small Country Houses*. Viking, London, 1988
SCHINZ, Marina, *Visions of Paradise: Themes and Variation on the Garden*. Thames and Hudson, London, 1985
SCOTT-JAMES, Anne, *Sissinghurst: The Making of a Garden*. Michael Joseph, London, 1975
STEEN, Nancy, *The Charm of Old Roses*. A.H. & A.W. Reed, 1966
STONES, Ellis, *Australian Garden Design*, Macmillan, Melbourne, 1971
SQUIRE, David, *The Scented Garden*, Doubleday, Australia, 1989
SUDELL, Richard, *Landscape Gardening*. Ward, Lock & Co, London and Melbourne, 1933
TANNER, Howard & BEGG, Jane, *The Great Gardens of Australia* Macmillan, Melbourne, 1976
——, *Converting the Wilderness: The Art of Gardening in Colonial Australia*, Australian Gallery Directors Council, Sydney, 1979

TAYLOR, Patrick, *Planting in Patterns*. Pavilion Books in association with The National Trust, London, 1989
THOMAS, Graham Stuart, *Shrub Roses of Today*. Phoenix House, London, 1962
——, *The Old Shrub Roses*. Phoenix House, 1955,
——, *A Garden of Roses*. Pavilion Books Ltd, UK, 1987
TOLLEY, Emelie & MEAD, Chris, *Herbs*. Sidgwick & Jackson, London, 1985
VEREY, Rosemary, *The Garden in Winter*. Frances Lincoln, 1988
WALLING, Edna, *Gardens in Australia*. Oxford University Press, Melbourne, 1946
——, *A Gardener's Log*. Anne O'Donovan, Melbourne, 1985
——, *The Edna Walling Book of Australian Garden Design*. Anne O'Donovan, 1981
——, *Country Roads: The Australian Roadside*. Pioneer Design Studio, 1985
——, *On the Trail of Australian Wildflowers*. Mulini Press, Canberra, 1984
WATTS, Peter, *The Gardens of Edna Walling*. National Trust of Victoria, 1982
WILSON, Glen, *Landscaping with Australian Plants*. Nelson, Melbourne, 1975
WHITE, Katharine, *Onward and Upward in the Garden* (6th edn.). McGraw-Hill Ryerson, Toronto, 1981 New York 1987

PHOTOGRAPHIC NOTES

TITLE PAGE: ~ *Wisteria at Boortkoi* ~ (Trisha Dixon)
CONTENTS: ~ *Hostas beside lake* ~ (Lorna Rose)
vii ~ *Wild garden, Bobundara* ~ (Trisha Dixon)
x ~ *Seat at Woomargama Station* ~ (Trisha Dixon)
2 ~ *Autumn at Hazeldean* ~ (Trisha Dixon)
3 ~ *Garden at Tocal, Paterson, NSW* ~ (Lorna Rose)
4 ~ *Red japonica* ~ (Lorna Rose)
5 ~ *Rural scene, England* ~ (Paul Clarke)
6 ~ *Shady terrace at Hazeldean* ~ (Trisha Dixon)
7 ~ *Left: Mossy path at Durroll* ~ (Trisha Dixon)
~ *Right: Rustic gate* ~ (Paul Foley)
8 AND 9 ~ *Woomargama Station* ~ (Trisha Dixon)
10–11 ~ *Daffodils at Banongil* ~ (Trisha Dixon)
12 ~ *Foxgloves and salvia* ~ (Lorna Rose)
13 ~ *Pastoral scene, England* ~ (Paul Clarke)
14 ~ *Wild garden at Bobundara* ~ (Trisha Dixon)
15 ~ *Buttercups, England* ~ (Paul Clarke)
16 ~ *Tocal homestead, Paterson, NSW* ~ (Lorna Rose)
17 ~ *Achillea in mist* ~ (Trisha Dixon)
18–19 ~ *Daffodils at Langley Vale* ~ (Trisha Dixon)
20 ~ *Iris at Kiah Lake* ~ (Trisha Dixon)
21 ~ *Picket gate at Tocal* ~ (Lorna Rose)
22 ~ *View from Pejar Park garden* ~ (Trisha Dixon)
23 ~ *Langley Vale driveway* ~ (Trisha Dixon)
24 ~ *Kiah Lake stables* ~ (Trisha Dixon)
25 ~ *Bucki garden* ~ (Trisha Dixon)
26 ~ *Bungarabee garden* ~ (Trisha Dixon)
27 ~ *Mt Annan entrance doorway* ~ (Trisha Dixon)
28 ~ *Left: Kiah Lake* ~ (Trisha Dixon)
~ *Right: Mt Annan courtyard* ~ (Trisha Dixon)
29 ~ *Garden room, Heide garden* ~ (Lorna Rose)
30–31 ~ *The Grisons, Switzerland* ~ (International Photographic Library)
32 ~ *Country driveway, England* ~ (Paul Clarke)
33 ~ *Entrance to driveway, England* ~ (Lorna Rose)
34 ~ *Creek crossing at Bobundara* ~ (Trisha Dixon)
35 ~ *Entrance at Brownlow Hill* ~ (Trisha Dixon)
36 ~ *Valerian at Manar* ~ (Trisha Dixon)
37 ~ *Micalago Station* ~ (Trisha Dixon)
38 ~ *Top: Brownlow Hill stables* ~ (Trisha Dixon)
~ *Below: Stables at Hazeldean* ~ (Trisha Dixon)
39 ~ *Painted Barn, U.S.A.* ~ (Paul Clarke)
40 ~ *Old Avon Lake homestead* ~ (Trisha Dixon)
41 ~ *Rustic building, Somerset* ~ (Lorna Rose)
42 ~ *Brownlow Hill urn* ~ (Trisha Dixon)
43 ~ *Roman garden at Clunie* ~ (Trisha Dixon)
44 ~ *Top: Garden Pool, England* ~ (Lorna Rose)
~ *Bottom: Water-loving plants* ~ (Lorna Rose)
45 ~ *Top: Lake at Shirley garden* ~ (Trisha Dixon)
~ *Bottom: Woomargama Station lake* ~ (Trisha Dixon)
46 ~ *Bucki garden* ~ (Trisha Dixon)
47 ~ *Nepeta and roses at Beechworth* ~ (Lorna Rose)
48 ~ *Window at Manar* ~ (Trisha Dixon)
49 ~ *Silver Moon rose at Nareen* ~ (Lorna Rose)
50 ~ *Courtyard at Bobundara* ~ (Trisha Dixon)
51 ~ *Rose arch at Bucki* ~ (Trisha Dixon)
52 ~ *Leafy path at Mawarra* ~ (Trisha Dixon)
53 ~ *Wild garden at Boortkoi* ~ (Trisha Dixon)
54 ~ *Fritillaries at Great Dixter* ~ (Lorna Rose)
55 ~ *Seat in Manar garden* ~ (Trisha Dixon)
56 ~ *Bridge in Coolringdon garden* ~ (Trisha Dixon)
57 ~ *Wild garden, Victoria* ~ (Joy Harland)
58 ~ *Hazelnut walk at Waiwere* ~ (Trisha Dixon)
59 ~ *Poppies and olive trees in Provence* ~ (David Barnes, Stockshots)
60–61 ~ *Maffra garden under snow* ~ (Trisha Dixon)
62 ~ *Hedge pattern, England* ~ (Paul Clarke)
63 ~ *Left: Vista at Powis* ~ (Lorna Rose)
~ *Right: Yew hedging at Powis Castle* ~ (Lorna Rose)
64 ~ *Left: Lambrigg garden* ~ (Trisha Dixon)
~ *Right: Parterre at Woomargama Station* ~ (Trisha Dixon)
65 ~ *Wisteria walk at Clunie* ~ (Trisha Dixon)
66 ~ *Left: Path at Heide* ~ (Lorna Rose)
~ *Right: Woomargama Station* ~ (Trisha Dixon)
67 ~ *Left: Woolongoon garden* ~ (Trisha Dixon)
~ *Right: Heide Kitchen garden* ~ (Lorna Rose)
68 ~ *Beaumauris garden* ~ (Trisha Dixon)
69 ~ *Tiled edging in Maffra garden* ~ (Trisha Dixon)
70 ~ *Avenue of Chestnuts, England* ~ (International Photographic Library)
71 ~ *Left: Elm driveway at Coolringdon* ~ (Trisha Dixon)
~ *Right: Victorian Kitchen garden, Chilton* ~ (Lorna Rose)
72 ~ *Pleached maple walk at Clunie* ~ (Trisha Dixon)
73 ~ *Entrance drive, England* ~ (Paul Clarke)
74 ~ *Hedge in Maffra garden* ~ (Trisha Dixon)
75 ~ *Great Dixter garden, England* ~ (Lorna Rose)

76 ~ *Hedge along waterway, England* ~ (Paul Clarke)
77 ~ *Herbaceous border at Powis* ~ (Lorna Rose)
78 ~ *Left: Historic Lanyon garden* ~ (Trisha Dixon)
~ *Right: Rose hedge at Kiah Lake* ~ (Trisha Dixon)
79 ~ *Nareen garden* ~ (Lorna Rose)
80–81 ~ *Heide Kitchen garden* ~ (Lorna Rose)
82 ~ *Perennial border at Powis Castle* ~ (Lorna Rose)
83 ~ *Achillea, Powys* ~ (Lorna Rose)
84 ~ *Left: Foxgloves at Manar* ~ (Trisha Dixon)
~ *Right: Perennial border at Bungarabee* ~ (Trisha Dixon)
85 ~ *Spring in Bucki Garden* ~ (Trisha Dixon)
86 ~ *Garden in August, Powis* ~ (Lorna Rose)
87 ~ *Ancient Yew hedges at Powis* ~ (Lorna Rose)
88 ~ *Top: Spring border at Bungarabee* ~ (Trisha Dixon)
~ *Below: Late afternoon at Dunraven* ~ (Trisha Dixon)
89 ~ *Pathway at Woomargama Station* ~ (Trisha Dixon)
90 ~ *Walled garden, Capel Manor, England* ~ (Lorna Rose)
91 ~ *Flower Border, Dora* ~ (Lorna Rose)
92 ~ *Heide garden* ~ (Lorna Rose)
93 ~ *Penelope rose, Heide garden* ~ (Lorna Rose)
94 ~ *Bobundara garden* ~ (Trisha Dixon)
95 ~ *Heide garden* ~ (Lorna Rose)
96 ~ *Roses at Kongbool* ~ (Lorna Rose)
97 ~ *Picket fence at Heide* ~ (Lorna Rose)
98 ~ *Mermaid Rose* ~ (Trisha Dixon)
99 ~ *Doorway into Mt Annan garden* ~ (Trisha Dixon)
100 ~ *Honeyflow Rose* ~ (Trisha Dixon)
101 ~ *Rosa Mundi Rose, Beaumaris* ~ (Trisha Dixon)
102 ~ *Daffodils at Banongil* ~ (Trisha Dixon)
103 ~ *Autumn at Hazeldean* ~ (Trisha Dixon)
104 ~ *Woomargama Station* ~ (Trisha Dixon)
105 ~ *Dog kennel at Bobundara* ~ (Trisha Dixon)
106 ~ *Beech trunks, England* ~ (Paul Clarke)
107 ~ *Spring ponds garden* ~ (Trisha Dixon)
108 ~ *Picket fence, Heide garden* ~ (Lorna Rose)
110 ~ *Mt Annan* ~ (Trisha Dixon)
111 ~ *Ha-ha at Mt Annan* ~ (Trisha Dixon)
112 ~ *Woomargama Station Ha-ha* ~ (Trisha Dixon)
113 ~ *Ha-ha at Woomargama* ~ (Trisha Dixon)
114 ~ *Stone wall, Kellie Castle, Scotland* ~ (Lorna Rose)
115 ~ *Kiah Lake garden* ~ (Trisha Dixon)
~ *Right: Stone walls at Boomey* ~ (Trisha Dixon)
116 ~ *Boomey garden* ~ (Trisha Dixon)
117 ~ *Bunratty Park, Eire* ~ (International Photographic Library)

118 ~ *Powis, Wales* ~ (Lorna Rose)
119 ~ *Heide front garden* ~ (Lorna Rose)
120 ~ *Aubretia in brick wall* ~ (Lorna Rose)
121 ~ *Spring blossom* ~ (Lorna Rose)
122 ~ *Woodstock side garden* ~ (Trisha Dixon)
123 ~ *Heide garden* ~ (Lorna Rose)
124 ~ *Erigeron at Pagan Park* ~ (Lorna Rose)
125 ~ *Maitland cottage garden* ~ (Lorna Rose)
126 ~ *Eyre Cottage herb garden* ~ (Trisha Dixon)
127 ~ *Rose cottage, Beechworth* ~ (Trisha Dixon)
128 ~ *Herbs drying at Bobundara* ~ (Trisha Dixon)
130 ~ *Apple orchard at Great Dixter* ~ (Lorna Rose)
131 ~ *Weacombe House, England* ~ (Lorna Rose)
132 ~ *Preserves at Bobundara* ~ (Trisha Dixon)
133 ~ *Apple trees* ~ (Joy Harland)
134 ~ *Meadow in Spring, Great Dixter* ~ (Lorna Rose)
135 ~ *Kitchen garden, England* ~ (Lorna Rose)
136 ~ *Heide Kitchen garden* ~ (Lorna Rose)
137 ~ *Birchfield Herbs* ~ (Trisha Dixon)
138 ~ *Herb garden at Banongil* ~ (Trisha Dixon)
139 ~ *Herbs drying at Bobundara* ~ (Trisha Dixon)
140 ~ *Birchfield Herbs* ~ (Trisha Dixon)
141 ~ *Kitchen garden, Kellie Castle, Scotland* ~ (Lorna Rose)
142 ~ *Waiwere no-dig vegetables* ~ (Trisha Dixon)
143 ~ *Kitchen garden, Chilton Foliat, England* ~ (Lorna Rose)
144 ~ *Vegetable garden at Dunraven* ~ (Trisha Dixon)
145 ~ *Weacombe House, England* ~ (Lorna Rose)
146 ~ *Globe artichokes, Lanyon* ~ (Trisha Dixon)
148 ~ *Old copper at Spring Ponds* ~ (Trisha Dixon)
149 ~ *Geese in Springwell courtyard* ~ (Trisha Dixon)
150 ~ *Beyond the garden fence at Beaumauris* ~ (Trisha Dixon)
151 ~ *Leaf mulch at Bobundara* ~ (Trisha Dixon)
152 ~ *Kitchen garden at Weacombe House* ~ (Lorna Rose)
153 ~ *Weacombe House, England* ~ (Lorna Rose)
154 ~ *Traveller's Rest Kitchen garden* ~ (Trisha Dixon)
155 ~ *Victorian Kitchen garden* ~ (Lorna Rose)
156 ~ *Wool clip at Bucki* ~ (Trisha Dixon)
157 ~ *Lavender walk at Bobundara* ~ (Trisha Dixon)
Jacket ~ *Country field with gate* ~ (The Photo Library)

INDEX